On Agoraphobia

Graham Caveney is a freelance writer. He has written on music and fiction for the *NME*, the *Face* and the *Independent*. He is the author of three previous books, including *The Boy With The Perpetual Nervousness*, which was longlisted for the PEN Ackerley Prize, and shortlisted for the Portico Prize.

Also by Graham Caveney

The Boy with the Perpetual Nervousness

'Never less than completely absorbing, simply because [Caveney] is such a nimble, exact writer, able to move swiftly but unjarringly between daft jokes and serious reflections.'
The Daily Telegraph

'Intellectually curious, emotionally bracing and immensely erudite . . . bright and funny, and full of telling quotes . . . it will hearten people who have agoraphobia, enlighten medics and teach outsiders all the lessons Caveney has learned.' Blake Morrison, *The Guardian*

'A strange and many-headed work that melds personal experience with cultural criticism . . . thoughtful, humane and unjustly enjoyable.' *The Sunday Times*

'One of my favourite living writers: intelligent, lucid and, most impressive of all, funny – even when he's writing about the most difficult subjects.' Jonathan Coe

'Captivating . . . but also a book unscared of open white space, which feels like an act of defiance. For a book about agoraphobia it covers a huge amount of ground.'
Richard Beard

'Graham Caveney approaches the subject of agoraphobia diaristically, legally, and philosophically; he drinks about it, reads about it, has therapy about it, and assembles the long and fascinating history of its writers.' Sarah Manguso

'A witty and engaging cultural history, and a frank and insightful memoir: *On Agoraphobia* is original, smart and hugely entertaining.' David Nicholls

On Agoraphobia

GRAHAM CAVENEY

PICADOR

First published 2022 by Picador

This paperback edition first published 2023 by Picador
an imprint of Pan Macmillan
The Smithson, 6 Briset Street, London EC1M 5NR
EU representative: Macmillan Publishers Ireland Ltd, 1st Floor,
The Liffey Trust Centre, 117–126 Sheriff Street Upper,
Dublin 1, D01 YC43
Associated companies throughout the world
www.panmacmillan.com

ISBN 978-1-529-05772-0

1 3 5 7 9 8 6 4 2

A CIP catalogue record for this book is available from the British Library.

Typeset by Palimpsest Book Production Ltd, Falkirk, Stirlingshire

Printed and bound by CPI Group (UK) Ltd, Croydon, CR0 4YY

Visit **www.picador.com** to read more about all our books
and to buy them. You will also find features, author interviews and
news of any author events, and you can sign up for e-newsletters
so that you're always first to hear about our new releases.

For Emma

'Autobiography has to do with time, with sequence and with what makes up the continuous flow of life. Here, I am talking of a space, of moments and discontinuities.'

Walter Benjamin, *One Way Street*

'It almost seemed that while he himself was marking out lines and courses on the wrinkled charts, some invisible pencil was also tracing lines and courses upon the deeply marked chart of his forehead.'

Herman Melville, *Moby-Dick*

'A bend in the road, and the whole place disappeared.'

Katherine Mansfield, 'The Woman at the Store'

On Agoraphobia

Nowhere

'We live in our own souls as in an unmapped region.'

Edith Wharton, *The Touchstone*

Thirty-plus years we've been together and still I don't know you. Intimate stranger, phantom limb, as unreachable as you are familiar. You have sculpted my desires, my ambitions, been a mockery of the free will I was always told I had. I cannot think without you. You are that which I cannot not know. You aspire to tyranny, a modus non-operandi.

You and me, baby, we're a neurotic two-step.

Agoraphobia. I want to write the word in the middle of the page, leave it stranded, surrounded with nothing but icy white space. My attempt at revenge. From the Greek 'agora' meaning 'marketplace', 'phobos' meaning 'fear'. The translation doesn't quite cut it. I baulk at its limitations. An insufficient word for a condition of insufficiency.

On Agoraphobia

What is *here* and what is *there*: the geography should be simple enough.

Yours.   Mine.

The gap is as wide as the space bar on a keyboard.

So why do you not work like that?

You did not come to me overnight. Like any stealthy lover you took it slowly. A block of time both dramatic and banal. You introduced me to fear, fear became aversion and aversion contorted itself into the core of who I am. It was subtle and unstoppable. Like surf drifting up the shore.

And then one day I realised I was too afraid to leave the house and I heard the word and realised it was being used about me.

Agoraphobia, my zero sign. Signifying everything.

Tell people you are claustrophobic and they touch your arm and nod in sympathy, maybe share a respectable neurosis of their own. They tell you they too have difficulty with lifts, the Tube, basements. They share your pain, flattered that you should trust them with an admission of vulnerability.

They may even like you more, read claustrophobia as a symptom of sensitivity, an extension of the artistic temperament.

Tell people you're agoraphobic and it brings the conversation to a standstill. They become uncomfortable. You have overstepped the mark (ironic, given the fear is precisely that). It is a vulnerability too far, one that needs to be spoken through tight lips, with lowered eyes. *I am agoraphobic*. It is not a sentence to be taken lightly, casually tossed into conversation.

It is less a confidence than a confession, a coming out.

A few years back one of my more ambitious shrinks asked me how I would go about teaching a course on agoraphobia. To pretend it was a transferable skill. This is what I wrote:

How To Be Agoraphobic

Avoid spaces that make you feel empty.

Avoid empty spaces.

Start to suspect there are two things only: indoors or outdoors.

On Agoraphobia

Find it surprising there are people in the world who are not agoraphobic.

Think of the windowpane as a movie screen.

Wonder if blind people can be agoraphobic.

Picture these words written on a flipchart.

Flip them.

And watch them disappear.

There was a time when the *agora* referred to an actual place, a forum for trade and exchange. That forum is now as big as the world. Not just the high street, the shopping mall, the retail park. But the screen in our bedrooms, the phone in our pocket, the chip beneath our skin. The agora is our *Geist*. The ubiquitous barcode, the self-service checkout.

Self service, a self checking out. In the feverish endgame of neoliberal capitalism it is difficult to distinguish a phobia of the marketplace from a phobia of life itself.

Hikikomori, the Japanese call it, the word both adjective and noun. It refers to acute social withdrawal and usually occurs in late (mostly male) adolescence. *Hikikomori* tend to have been bullied at school or dropped out from university. They live by the light of computer terminals, glutted on video games and takeaway food. Tamaki Saito – who first coined the term – estimates there are over a million sufferers, noting that the shame attached to the condition makes numbers difficult to gauge.

Some sufferers in their forties have been isolated for twenty years or more. The Japanese Cabinet Office refer to them as *first-generation hikikomori* – bracing themselves for the generations yet to come.

Attempts at describing agoraphobia seem to rely upon the failure to do so – make inadequacy part of its constitution so to speak. It seems intent on evading capture, refusing to be confined to anything so mundane as a definition. The case studies are replete with subclauses, exceptions, inconsistencies. Testimonies are hesitant and slippery, inaccurate the moment they get spoken. As though a falling short is part of the diagnostic process. *Under-inclusivity*, the psychiatrists call it.

The condition is fugitive, it smuggles itself in via other categories of mental illness. It is allied to depression, addiction, obsessive ritual. They are like best friends trying on each other's clothes, assembling outfits from their collective wardrobe of symptoms. It is amazing how many combinations are available: free-floating, seasonally affected, weather-specific. A bottomless well.

'Agoraphobia is not only a matter of marketplaces', wrote one medic in 1899, 'but also of any unhelpful space, – of a space, that is, in which there are no easy steps for the eye.'

A scopic-spatial dread then; connected with vision and locomotion. A drama of exposure, uncertain movement and thresholds. As porous as fog, yet pinprick precise.

A 'fear of space, of the void', wrote Henri Legrand de Saulle, a French psychiatrist, in 1878: 'Not only in the street but also in the theatre, in church, on an upper floor, at a window going onto a large courtyard or looking over the countryside, in an omnibus, a ferry or on a bridge . . . He feels as if he is destroyed . . . trembles in all his limbs, grows pale, shivers, blushes, is covered with sweat, grows more and more alarmed, can hardly stand up on his tottering legs . . . If one's gaze were suddenly to be plunged into a deep gulf, if one were to imagine being suspended above a fiery crater, to be crossing the Niagara on a rigid cord or feel that one was rolling into a precipice, the resulting impression could be no more painful, more terrifying, than that provoked by the fear of spaces.'

Agoraphobia disrupts our metaphors, sabotages The Journey we are all supposed to be on. *I'm getting there, I'm at a crossroads, taking a detour, a fork in the road, an uphill struggle, the right track, the straight and narrow, all downhill from here.* My neurosis makes the language of topography stutter.

The writer George Perec once expressed surprise that people wear watches but never compasses.

I've tried to write you many times and each time you wanted to go someplace else. You are vain and lofty, scornful of anything so vulgar as a beginning, middle and end. You are fragile and suspicious, worried that writing will expose your essential absurdity.

Imagine this written around the edges of the page. A book consisting of nothing but margins.

Trace

'The map? I will first make it.'

Patrick White, *Voss*

The first book I fell in love with had an agoraphobe as its hero, although I didn't think of him as either at the time. To my twelve-year-old eyes Boo Radley was simply *To Kill A Mockingbird*'s oddball, the one who saves Scout. I never stopped to think about just how singularly freakish a character he is. When Scout asks if it's true that Boo is kept chained to a bed, Atticus answers, 'There are other ways of making people into ghosts.'

A *malevolent phantom* is how the children think of him, thrilling to their descriptions of his yellow teeth, popped eyes and diet of raw squirrels.

Back then agoraphobes were other people.

If we're talking agoraphobia, we're talking books. I slip between their covers, lose myself in the turn of one page, re-discover myself on the next. Reading is a game of hide-and-seek.

Narrative and neurosis, uneasy bedfellows sleeping top to toe. They conspire, entangle, seduce and sustain each other. Ask me how I am and the answer will depend on the book I am reading. On the sentences I am being fed.

Libraries and second-hand bookshops are my natural habitat, castles of interiority. 'Literature,' wrote Lorrie Moore, 'is the correspondence of two agoraphobics. It is lonely and waited for, brilliant and pure and frightened, a marriage of birds, a conversation of the blind.'

The story goes that in 1654 the philosopher Blaise Pascal was thrown from his horse whilst crossing the bridge at Neuilly-sur-Seine. It is said that thereafter he sensed an abyss on his left side and required a chair beside him to prevent his falling into it. This story probably isn't true.

Two hundred years later Baudelaire would revisit the story in his poem 'The Abyss':

'All around me the brink, the depths, the space

On Agoraphobia

'I'm spellbound, petrified, held fast in place.'

Modernity would find a peculiar home in its accelerated heart for the agoraphobe. Even as it produced him.

'The archetypal modern man', wrote Marshall Berman in *All That Is Solid Melts Into Air*, 'is a pedestrian thrown into the maelstrom of modern city traffic, a man alone contending against an agglomeration of mass and energy that is heavy, fast and lethal. The burgeoning street and boulevard traffic knows no spatial or temporal bounds, spills over into every urban space, imposes its tempo on everybody's time, transforms the whole environment into moving chaos.'

As a medical category, the agoraphobe was a product of the nineteenth-century city. Both illness and metropolis were the result of unprecedented change, transformation at a speed that was dizzying, turbulent and seemingly boundless. Steam engines, railroads, industrial zones, factories, newspapers, telephones, telegraphs, trades unions, nation states, multinational companies, the move from the rural to the urban.

Cities were places of promiscuous intermingling: of classes, ethnicities, genders. The world's largest marketplace avant la lettre.

If the flâneur embraced the disorientation of urban life, the agoraphobe proved a more reluctant assimilationist. Both were responses to Modernity's intoxicating canvas – the flâneur's as promise, the agoraphobe's as threat.

Time compressed, space warped and expanded. The sheer proximity of unruly bodies. Transit brought about a new way of being, new forms of writing.

Writers were responding not to patrons or nature or God, but to the vertiginous demands of geography.

Traffic and transport would became the muses of Modernity, tropes of immanence and anomie: the car crash which opens Musil's *The Man Without Qualities*, the carriage carrying Joyce's Stephen Dedalus to Paddy Dignam's funeral, the apparition of faces in Pound's famous Metro.

'It's not catastrophes, murders, deaths, diseases, that age and kill us,' wrote Virginia Woolf in *Mrs Dalloway*, 'it's the way people look and laugh, and run up the steps of omnibuses.'

Say the word *agoraphobic* and a whole template of manner is conjured up. Maybe a minor character from a domestic novel. Surreptitious fringe, hesitant speech, weak hand-shake. Prone to blushing, no eye contact, hug-averse.

On Agoraphobia

When Anita Brookner's Lewis Percy meets his future wife, she tells him she calls herself Tissy: 'My real name's Patricia, really. Patricia Harper. When I was little I couldn't say Patricia, so I called myself Tissy, and the name's stuck. I get called it all the time now.'

She is that curious and eerie figure: the woman frozen in girlhood. Agoraphobia has made her a terminal adolescent, furtive and sulky, refusing to leave home.

They meet in a library, where else?

' "A Tragedy, that girl," remarks Tissy's boss: "Agoraphobia . . . Says she can't go out alone. Her mother brings her in the morning, collects her for lunch, brings her back at two, and collects her again in the evening. I've tried to talk to her, but to no avail. Apparently it came on with adolescence, although I believe there was some family trouble as well. The father," she said, lowering her voice.'

Agoraphobia dominates their marriage, becomes its structuring absence. She is a spatial anorexic, a home-bound Bartleby. Tissy prefers not to, although her phobia never feels like a preference. She embodies a steely passivity, turns spontaneity to ash.

In *The Inheritors*, his novel of 1901, Ford Madox Ford's narrator feels he has entered a fourth dimension: 'All around me stretched an immense town – an immense blackness,' says Arthur Granger: 'People – thousands of people hurried past me – had errands, had aims, had others to talk to, to trifle with. But I had nobody. This immense city, this immense blackness, had no interiors for me. There were house fronts, staring windows, closed doors, but nothing within: no rooms, no hollow places.'

Ford's biographer Max Saunders calls him Ford's 'first fictional agoraphobic'.

The fictional agoraphobic – it's a phrase that has stayed with me for years, the title of the novel I will never write.

I imagine writing it in chalk.

Vessels

'Inside everyone, is there an anxious person who
stands to hesitate in an empty room?'

Elizabeth Bowen, *The Death of the Heart*

I grew up with a whole mythology of nerves. They had
their own poetics. *Bad with his nerves, a bundle of nerves,
a nervous wreck.* Nerves were a site of catastrophe. I used
to picture an army of ants living just beneath the skin,
patrolling the blood vessels. They were in charge of tickling, itching, reflexes.

My childish fantasies had a venerable ancestry. For centuries our understanding of nerves was indebted to the
second-century Greek physician Galen, for whom the nervous system was the key to maximum health. He thought of
nerves as channels for animal spirits.

In Lancashire nerves were the reason people *ended up in Brockhall*. It was one of the earliest taunts I heard growing up, a bogeyman.

Your parents met in Brockhall.

You were born in Brockhall.

You're going to die in Brockhall.

Near a small village on the outskirts of Blackburn, Brockhall Hospital was one of Europe's largest mental institutions. It had been built in 1904, a Reformatory for Inebriate Women. To be admitted a woman had to be convicted of drunkenness at least four times in one year. In 1924 it expanded its remit and established itself as an institution for 'mental defectives'.

Fifty years later it no longer used those words. But by then it had become a playground jeer.

Brockhall Hospital was an Edwardian invention, a sign of enlightened progress. It was an announcement: *Just look at how far we have come, Victorian values have been left behind.*

On Agoraphobia

The Victorians believed we are born with a finite amount of *nerve force* – an amount appropriate to our social status. On the balance sheet of work and family, duty and pleasure, they are assets. They must never become liabilities. Nerves are our net worth. Spend them wisely.

A nervous economy, and the economy of nerves. Surely a model that is with us still. In his 1874 guide *The Maintenance of Health* the physician and medical writer J. Milner Fothergill wrote that 'Man has a reserve of force: like the balance of a prudent firm at its bankers . . . If this is too far drawn upon, a sudden demand becomes a very serious matter.'

A nervous breakdown is bankruptcy, a form of fiscal and psychic panic.

I often heard the word *panic* in history lessons, used to describe the various economic crises that had gripped the West throughout the nineteenth century. They seemed to come roughly twenty years apart – 1819, 1837, 1857, 1873 – but continued to take people by surprise. We were taught they were brought about by the growing inter-connectedness of the global market. All were followed by periods of economic depression.

Depression, nerves, panic. I was taught to be phobic about the words themselves, as though saying them out loud would conjure the things into being. Life was hard enough without people finding new things to be frightened of.

Our lexicon of nerves was slangy, semi-comedic. We used the word 'skryke' for 'cry' – a term reserved mainly for women and children. It signalled indulgence, emotional illegitimacy. It was often the prelude to being given something to skryke about.

Suspicious of the inner life, our language equated emotion with dangerous excess. Emotions were soggy. Too many of them left you wet, a big girl. We talked of fretting, being *mardy*, worrying about *nowt*. We talked of *mithering* (a form of mothering gone wrong?).

The sensitive, the delicate, the timid? They simply *didn't know they were born*. So said people nostalgic for the days of National Service.

And for the mad, the disturbed, the not-quite-right, a vocabulary that relied on the cartoonish comedy of popular culture: *Looney Tunes, fruit the loop, Loopy Lou*. Worlds of deranged childhood.

On Agoraphobia

At various points in my adult life (why do I want to say so-called?) I've had to move back in with my parents. It was, to say the least, far from ideal. My father was baffled by my phobia, suspicious that a fear of empty space was actually a fear of hard work. He may well have been right, although it was not the work, but the *going out* to do it that turned my bowels to water.

My father embodied all the virtues of working-class masculinity: resilience and silent strength, virtues that in the 1970s and 80s were becoming less virtuous than they once were. He was an endangered species, like those polar bears on melting ice caps.

His favourite movies were Westerns, stories of frontier virtue, bravery against the odds. We used to sit and watch *The Searchers* every time it was on TV, would silently thrill to John Wayne bringing Natalie Wood back to her family.

It was the Duke walking away at the end that did it.

Ask him about his job and he will look at you like you are daft. It was work. Work was work. He did it because they paid him to do it. And then he came home.

Work was something you went out to do.

He was a groundsman at the local comprehensive – the place I was headed had I not made it to the Catholic grammar school.

I was headed for a bigger world.

We were raised to know our place – somewhere with a built-in desire to get to a better place.

Whilst never forgetting the place you came from.

That's a lot of *places* and a lot of *nots*.

Spaces where I don't know my place.

Is this why I am agoraphobic?

Onset

'And yet, something came again, which took me
like paper, crumpled me up and threw me away;
something unprecedented.'

Rainer Maria Rilke, *The Notebooks of
Malte Laurids Brigge*

In Sue Townsend's 1982 play *Bazaar & Rummage* a social
worker tells her client: You've got to face up to it sooner or
later . . . Whatever it is that's keeping you in.

We know what it is, it's agoraphobia, says the client.

That came second, says the social worker, what came
first?

Agoraphobia is not so much a fear of going out as a fear of
something dreadful happening whilst being out.

And in order for that dreadful thing to happen, something dreadful must have already happened.

The phobia knows what it is avoiding, even though the phobic may not.

Psychologists call it *the originary drama*.

In 2014 the singer Alison Moyet discussed her agoraphobia on Radio 4's *Desert Island Discs*. She had gone to see Elvis Costello, a musical hero, and had been invited to an after-show party. 'There he was and he was lovely. He was charming and I wanted to say to him You Were Wonderful and had all these wonderful descriptions of him. What came out of my mouth was, You dragged that out a bit, didn't you? Once I did that, I just felt, I don't trust myself in polite society.'

The resulting agoraphobia kept her company for the next thirty years.

In *Return to Yesterday* – a memoir that reads like a mystery novel – Ford Madox Ford describes his first attack. His family had inherited an immense opal. A series of disasters – health, work, financial – struck after the inheritance. He became convinced the jewel was cursed and decided to rid himself of it. He donated it to a Catholic charity – the

On Agoraphobia

Little Sisters of the Poor: 'I handed it to the young woman in charge of registrations with an immense sigh of relief. Alas again: I had no sooner turned the corner of the post-office than I found myself almost completely unable to walk. Campden Hill Road assumed an aspect as steep as the side of the Righi. I could hardly drag my feet along. There began the long illness.'

Every agoraphobe's originary drama is different, but every agoraphobe is similar in their reaction to that drama. They – we – all share a belief, insistent and foreboding: *such a thing must never be allowed to happen again.*

Originary dramas do not get more dramatic than Edvard Munch's: 'I was walking along a path with two friends – the sun was setting – I felt a breath of melancholy – suddenly the sky turned blood red – I stopped and leaned against the railing deathly tired – looking out across flaming clouds that hung like blood and sword over the deep blue fjord and town – my friends walked on – I stood there trembling with anxiety and I felt a great, infinite scream through nature.'

So wrote Munch about the experience which lay behind his most famous painting.

When I was a student *The Scream* seemed to be everywhere. Or was that when I became an agoraphobic student?

I am on a coach on the M6. It is the mid-1980s and I am nineteen years old. I have been to my parents' for the Christmas vacation. Warwick University is my new home, although I'm not sure if you could use the word 'home' about somewhere I'd been for a mere four months.

The fear descended the same way the mist falls on Scafell Pike – as though it had been there all along, waiting in ambush.

It banishes all thoughts, insists that your body be governed by its most primal impulses.

I was suddenly at a funfair, an internal carnival whose control settings were not my own.

A rollercoaster lurch in the stomach, the tightening twirl of the solar plexus, an offbeat disco of the heart. A funless unfunny no fun funfair.

The Scream *was not just a poster on walls but could be found on key rings, beach balls, tote bags, coffee mugs. It was a way of turning angst into kitsch, of burying* The Scream *beneath its own iconography. The image itself, its vibrant shock, seemed irretrievably lost, made invisible by a million repeated viewings.*

Is it possible to have déjà vu and amnesia at the same time, to look around and not recognise anything whilst knowing you have felt this way before.

To be simultaneously falling and frozen?

Fear reminds you that you are still an infant, utterly helpless, nothing but a cluster of sensations. It has a hallucinatory quality, it renders you dim and insubstantial. The mind is in meltdown, trying to absent itself. No unity, coherence, solidity.

It feels like going mad.

It *is* going mad.

Panic is a pitbull with a rag doll. It churns up the intestines, gnaws and chews at the lungs and throat. It sets off an inner fire alarm; a piercing shriek getting louder by the second. The message is urgent and absolute. *You do not exist.*

De-personalisation, the shrinks would later call it.

'When emotion too far exceeds its cause', wrote the poet Elizabeth Bishop in 'The Map'. But what if emotion has no cause, is the site of its own excess? What happens when emotions descend without reason, take up residence in your body with no object other than themselves?

Panic is self-perpetuating, a feedback loop.

Panic begets panic.

Sweat begins swirling its way down the small of my back. Heart is hammering, blood pounding. I cannot breathe. I gasp, try to swallow. Gasp some more. My guts become a graveyard, my legs are made of plasticine. Electricity shoots through my fingers and feet, fireworks in my forehead. My sphincter threatens to betray me.

Munch's drama took place late in 1892 in Ekeberg east of Oslo (Kristiania as it was then). He had just returned to his native Norway having studied in Paris and Berlin. It had been an education in the avant-garde – an encounter with French Impressionism followed by an immersion in the bohemians who gathered around August Strindberg in the Black Piglet cafe.

On Agoraphobia

Nowhere to go, no place to hide. The other passengers stare, shuffle, whisper. They seem a long way away, even though they are all too close. The coach has no bathroom.

Through the window, car after car after car, the motorway a picture of horrifying symmetry. There is nowhere to shelter, nothing to keep me safe. My throat is constricted, tongue stuck like Velcro to the roof of my desert-dry mouth.

Cut to Manchester bus station, stumbling into the public toilets, sobbing and shouting in a cubicle. Too much breath now, can't stop it coming, breath like a whirlwind.

So why can't I breathe?

I kneel down, press my forehead against a cold porcelain bowl. I try to vomit but produce nothing but sour bile. I close my eyes, the smell of piss acting like smelling salts.

Eventually – fifteen, twenty minutes later? – I breathe, at last. Unlock the cubicle door.

Of his time as a student Munch's most exhaustive biographer Sue Prideaux writes: 'When he went outside he walked hugged up against the walls, afraid of walking in open space.'

I examine my reflection in the bathroom mirror, surprised to see the face that stares back: me and not me. My fingers caress the forehead, checking the contents of the skull are still on the inside.

I think: *Something terrible has happened.*

And: *Something terrible is about to happen.*

The Scream *figure's head is a lightbulb, its face a foetus. Its hands are shielding the ears. It is not the figure (she, he?) who is screaming, but nature itself. The skies are a feverish red, the fjord the colour of over-ripe plums.*

My world was dismantled in the space of forty minutes. I look again at the face in the mirror, splash cold water over it.

I feel I have signed a non-negotiable contract.

The Scream's *brushstrokes are gyrating, agitated, maniacal. There is a crisis in perspective, a disjunction between foreground and background. Two women float by on parasols.*

And the ghost of a question: how did the figure get home?

Fade

'To pass freely through open doors, it is necessary to respect the fact that they have solid frames.'

Robert Musil, *The Man Without Qualities*

Is that my agoraphobia talking? The sentence slips between thoughts as I recall my childhood, wonder if it was always thus.

We retrofit our memories, edit them to match the adults we become. I remember myself as a sickly child with a shock of blond curls and a dislike of other children. I remember myself as frightened.

My body felt like an unwieldy thing, awkward and out of sync. I would trip up, misjudge distances, bump into things. *You're all fingers and thumbs*, my teachers told me.

It took me years to tell my left from right. Even now – in my mid-fifties – I sometimes have to check my internal memo: *I write with my right.* I was baffled by tying shoelaces, scissors. Maps remain mysterious. I am still unable to pack a suitcase.

Dyspraxia, we would probably call it now. *Cack-handed* is what we called it then – from the Old English *cack* meaning dung.

The memories are all indoors, a modest terraced house with space enough to stage my dramas of sovereignty. The room beneath the stairs is a submarine, the spare room a fortress. My mother allows me to take my meals there, *anything for a quiet life* she says. I sit with a torch and read. *My Dens* I call them. Each has a different password.

I am an only child, undivided focus of my parents' interest, sole bearer of their expectations. It means both self-sufficiency and permanent scrutiny. I have no other children to teach me the rules of childhood.

An only child is almost a contradiction in terms.

I am unschooled in boundary disputes, no need to negotiate the shades of personal space. No siblings, no bunk beds, no calls for parental adjudication.

Mine. Not mine.

A clear-cut demarcation.

My mother would tell me to *go and play out*, to *get from under my feet*. I hear her advice as banishment, exile, skulk silently off to my den (password *Captain Scarlet*). She tells me, *It's a sin to be indoors on days like this*.

The streets outside my bedroom window were one giant playground. Walls had goal posts and cricket stumps chalked on them. Girls played hopscotch. Their skipping songs were hypnotic; uncanny nonsense verse. Out with my parents we would sing a nursery rhyme: *If you stand on a nick / You'll marry a brick / And a beetle will come to your wedding*.

Thus did we appease the spirits of the street.

My mother is the kind of northern working-class woman popular culture finds it hard to shake off. She is a staple of soap operas, sitcoms, kitchen-sink dramas. I grew up watching her scrub our front step, a totem for those about to enter the house.

A clean step was a sign of respectability. It demarcated the boundary between domestic and public space.

At university I would attend seminars with titles like 'Women Silenced' and 'Women Speak Out' and wonder where such muted women had been hiding. Certainly not in my hometown. There narrative authority belonged solely to women and was no less powerful for being called gossip by its men.

The woman who lived opposite would stand on her front step, cigarette in her cigarette holder, scandalously smoking for all the world to see. She is a divorcee, a peroxide blonde with a gentleman friend. *Who does she think she is?* my mother says, staring out the front window. *She's been round the block a few times*, my father answers.

Been round the block.

Streets were disreputable, unseemly. Places where people got up to all sorts.

I read fairy tales, devour them in the hope of becoming one. They are tales of confinement and transgression, things being out of place. Castles, imprisoned princesses, bears sleeping in the wrong bed.

I fall in love with the miller's daughter, locked in a tower spinning straw into gold.

On Agoraphobia

At thirteen I read Dickens' *Great Expectations*, am enraptured by the reclusive Miss Havisham. Rejected at the altar she in turn rejects the world. I picture her entombed in Satis House, cryogenically frozen in her wedding dress, the clocks all frozen at twenty to nine.

There seemed to me something magnificent about such bitterness, a spite so pure it is all-consuming. She is utterly self-contained, omnipotent in her exile.

When Pip first meets her he wonders at 'the vanity of sorrow which had become a master mania, like the vanity of penitence, the vanity of remorse, the vanity of unworthiness, and other monstrous vanities that have been curses in this world'.

Dickens leads to Wilkie Collins – *The Woman in White*, home to one of the most sinister grotesques of nineteenth-century fiction. Mr Fairlie is a man whose excessive sensitivity leads to a permanent migraine. He languishes in his room, able to tolerate only the dimmest of lights and the softest of sounds. His feet 'were effeminately small,' writes Collins, clad in 'little womanish bronze-leather slippers'.

At one point Fairlie describes himself as 'nothing but a bundle of nerves dressed up to look like a man.' His nerves have castrated him.

I too prefer stories to sunshine. Catholicism has no shortage of these. A hand so pure it must not know what the other hand is doing. Offending eyes plucked out. Devils sent raging into the bodies of swine. The raising of the dead. Such stories scorch themselves into the fibres of my being. St Augustine once said we do not kneel to pray, but that kneeling is the prayer itself. Thus does theology become anatomy.

The Catholic Church may be guilty of many things but lacking a definite structure is not one of them. Our Commandments are not called the Ten Suggestions. A cross, a trinity, the iconography of my immortal soul.

My first memory is of another kind of fairy tale. I am four years old and sat on my grandfather's knee. The whole family is there. Everyone is excited. On the TV screen in front of us men in car-tyre suits and white motorcycle helmets are planting an American flag. They are in what appears to be a coal-black desert. They are bouncing in slow motion. My grandfather tells me I will remember this when I'm older, that this is space.

And space is the future.

Mangle

'Phenomena which cannot otherwise be accounted for
are commonly attributed to nervousness – but to what
is nervousness attributable?'

James Manby Gully, *An Exposition of the Symptoms,*
Essential Nature and Treatment of Neuropathy, or
Nervousness (1837)

In Helen Dunmore's novel *Talking to the Dead* agoraphobia
becomes the key to other, much darker family secrets. It
is the story of two sisters, both haunted by memories of a
brother who died when they were young. One of them feels
unable to go further than her garden gate. 'Her face is so
calm that it would be impossible to guess how frightened
she is,' remarks her sister, 'unless you knew her.' The calm-
ness alarms her; a tranquil state in anyone else. Here a sign
of its opposite.

Agoraphobia can never be incidental. The sufferer is always assumed to be keeping something back.

They are getting ready to go out, their regular Friday night at the Catholic social club. My father smells of aftershave and tobacco, my mother of lipstick and sweet chalky face powder. They will meet other couples there. The men will drink pints of bitter, the women port and lemon. When they return they will be what they call merry. They will play records – The Dubliners, Jim Reeves, Faron Young's 'Four in the Morning'.

My father will loosen the tie on his starched white shirt and talk nostalgically about an Ireland he knows only through the memories of his own father.

My parents went to the same Catholic primary school, attended the same Catholic church. At the age of seventeen he took her home to meet his mother. She looked at my mum, turned to my dad and said, *So is she Catholic*. It was not a question.

I am getting ready for them to go out. I am old enough to look after myself. I am waiting for the doorbell, will read my new book whilst I wait. It is by a Jewish man who lived in Prague and wrote in German. His stories are nothing like fairy tales, even though they are about courts and castles and animals. He writes in the voice of an ape giving a report of his capture. He writes as a mouse, a dog, a mole. He writes about a man who wakes up as an insect. I dip into his diaries and read: *I am separated from all things by a hollow space.*

I am fourteen years old. I am finding out what grown-ups are like.

He is getting ready for them to go out. He will take off his black suit and dog collar, change into what he calls *civvies* – jeans, leather jacket, open-necked shirt. If he wasn't a Catholic priest you would think he was getting ready for a date.

This is not a memoir of abuse. Yet still I feel the need to acknowledge its presence, as though my agoraphobia doesn't make sense without it.

Assuming agoraphobia is something about which it is possible to make sense.

Vladimir Nabokov once told an interviewer that his most famous novel, *Lolita*, was prompted by a story he came across in a newspaper: 'As far as I can recall, the initial shiver of inspiration was somehow prompted by a newspaper story about an ape in the Jardin des Plantes, who, after months of coaxing by a scientist, produced the first drawing ever charcoaled by an animal: this sketch showed the bars of the poor creature's cage.'

Poor creature indeed.

I used to imagine how he had discovered his desires, if his religious vocation was a way of repressing or indulging them. Celibate priest as denial, or cover story? I know now it was the wrong question, that prisoners do not get to choose their jail.

Nabokov's gorilla, a pitiful image. Humbert drives Lolita across America, his prized possession kept docile with a diet of sweets and saccharine popular music. It is a road movie with no end in sight. They are in flight from the enquiries of concerned citizens, moving from motel to lonely motel, the road's wide-open spaces getting emptier by the day.

I used to wonder what his – my – cut-off point was going to be. If there was an age at which I would no longer be to his taste. Fifteen? Sixteen? Voice fully broken? I would wonder what he would do then, how he would break the news that my time was up.

On Agoraphobia

What was it like to watch me grow a little bit older every day? To see me approach my sell-by date.

To be sexually abused is to be invaded, colonised. It calls into question one of the key tenets of our selfhood: *Who does my body belong to?* The answer is far from clear. Strategies of survival include: collaboration, insurgency, separatism, insurrection. We may combine these strategies, or alternate them. We may go on dirty protest or hunger strike, or carve graffiti on our arms and the backs of our legs.

Or we may retreat, find the unexpectedness of society simply too much to risk.

I can see the emotional rationale. My most intimate boundaries were violated and thus do I mistrust boundaries. It's a crisis of coordinates, an inability to accept the shape of the world.

Except agoraphobia is not a crossword. Attempting to fill in the blanks tells me nothing about them other than they are impossible to fill.

I imagine a Venn diagram, its overlapping circles of abuse, agoraphobia and addiction. I was taught such diagrams showed all possible logical relations between *sets* – a set being a well-defined collection of distinct objects.

Agoraphobia reminds me of the limits of what I know, insists I remain its eternal student. It speaks a different language, operates by its own logic. A phobia is that which cannot be persuaded.

Saying

'A house is your third skin, after the skin made of
flesh and clothing.'

Jenny Erpenbeck, *Visitation*

Between 1978 and 1979 the Taiwanese-American artist
Tehching 'Sam' Hsieh embarked on the first of his 'One
Year Performances'. He called it *Cage Piece*. In the presence of a lawyer he locked himself inside an 11.5 × 9 × 8-
foot wooden cage in his apartment in New York, furnished
only with a single bed, bucket, wash basin and lights. He
shaved his head, pulled on a prison-style uniform and
lived in the cell a whole year. In an interview years later
he said the experience had made him realise: life is a
sentence.

Prison sentence, grammatical sentence?

I am fourteen years old. I inhabit a smaller version of myself, scrunched and permanently alert. I am no longer a teenager. I am the photograph of a teenager. My parents call it adolescence.

I do not call it anything.

I did not call it anything because there was no language available to do so. I was raised on a series of conversational ready-mades waiting to be rifled through like a rolodex. Language was a way of not speaking, of preventing things from being said.

I was told this was *telling it like it is.*

For two years my house was filled with an aching emptiness, one that rendered its usual chatter hollow and morbid. It became one of those puzzles you see in magazines: two pictures of what appears to be the same room and the question: Spot five things that are different.

And so we told it like it is.

Strong in th'arm, weak in t'head. We were keen to separate bodies and minds. I would watch men with sinewy forearms dig holes in the road and listen to their exchanges, the finely honed rhythms of obscenity and manual labour. They never missed a beat.

I never dared ask if the formula about strong arms and weak heads was reversible.

Or what happens if you are weak in both.

Hard work never hurt anyone. A statement belied on a weekly basis by accidents and fatalities; by the everyday evidence of missing limbs and scarred hands, the ghostly complexions and diminished lung capacities of everyone around us.

My hometown is a valley, funnel-shaped, the population poured in to meet the demands of the cotton trade. A trade now gone. *Post-industrial* is the word that gets used, a word that does not seem complete unless followed by *decline*.

There's always someone worse off than us. A sentiment particularly tailored to soothe the souls of the perennially hard done by. Other people's misery was oddly reassuring. A reminder that suffering is hierarchical, and we are not at the bottom of its pyramid.

These sayings spoke through us like a ventriloquist working his dummy, soldering themselves into the circuits of who we are and how we think. They were replacements for curiosity, balms for anger.

In *High Wages*, her novel about the Lancashire of 1912, Dorothy Whipple wrote of 'the brick, the stone, the grass, the very air deadened down to a general drab by the insidious filter of soot . . . It was no feeble trickling ugliness, but a strong, salient hideousness that was almost exhilarating.'

She wrote that in 1930. Fifty years later that *almost* was doing a lot of heavy lifting.

There's nowt so queer as folk. The daily mantra of my growing up, a way of registering otherness whilst closing it down. It's a statement of resigned bemusement. The queerness of folk was always the end of the discussion, never its starting point.

For his second 'One Year Performance' Hsieh punched a time clock on the hour every hour, twenty-four hours a day, for the whole of April 1980 – April 1981. Each clocking-in was photographed and later displayed with the punch cards in an art gallery in Australia. There were 8,763 cards on display, 133 short of the number taken. The gallery's curator commented: There is an element of failure built in to the work.

Picture

'We shall find that nervous ailments are no longer
confined to the better ranks in life, but rapidly
extending to the poorer classes.'

Thomas Trotter,
A View of the Nervous Temperament (1807)

She checks her bag and pockets. Keys, phone, purse, book,
water, packed lunch. She adds her waterproofs, just in case.
She – Emma – is going to catch a bus to Alderley Edge
on the outskirts of Manchester and walk for fifteen miles
around what is known as Cheshire's Golden Triangle. She
tells me there can be found some of the most beautiful
countryside in the North of England – a place with no shortage of contenders. She is excited, uses words like *restorative*,
peaceful, *bracing*. She tells me lots of people do this, that it
happens all the time.

They do. I remember now. I used to do this too. Walk in nature. Long ago. So long ago that the memory seems to be of someone I barely knew. But walk we did, me and my father, regularly, along the Bollin River, through Macclesfield Forest, up to Prestbury. I tend to forget (ignore, deny?) the more pastoral aspects of my childhood. Once there, agoraphobia insists it has always been there.

It has a scorched-earth policy towards personal history.

Emma jokes that my agoraphobia is an extension of being from Lancashire, the tight-knit community *in extremis*. She may be right. Is my phobia simply small-mindedness writ large, a catastrophic failure of the imagination? I grew up in a town with people who had never travelled the fifteen miles to the neighbouring town let alone the forty miles to Manchester. If they had, they would pronounce *there was nowt there when you got there*.

Other places, then, were places with nothing there.

I have now been agoraphobic for longer than not. It is difficult to remember that I have been anything else. Phobia becomes naturalised, even though nature (uninhabited, unsheltered) is one of the things I am most phobic about.

On Agoraphobia

The Pennines, the Lake District, Beacon Fells, Ribble Valley, Pendle Hill. The contours of my growing up, the names themselves moving poets to tears of egotistical sublimity. Nature was curative, the feather in our oft-derided cloth caps. It was our riposte to factory life; God's compensation for all that dreary, deafening, soul-deadening work.

There was a song I'd hear in the pubs: 'Manchester Rambler' by the Spinners, written by Ewan MacColl. 'I may be a wage slave on Monday', went the chorus, 'but I am a free man on Sunday.'

I can't help but wonder about the gap between the two lines. It's bigger than anyone's letting on.

Agoraphobia's soundtrack isn't folk music. It's glitchy electronica; distortion, feedback.

Agoraphobia is an assault on pastoral fantasy, the parody of a rustic Eden. No wonder it feels like blasphemy. The North was supposed to be the epitome of common sense, a place whose straight-talking wisdom is guaranteed by those clipped no-nonsense vowels. It's no place for bloody neurotics.

And should we add treason to the charge sheet, English pastoral being the height of patriotism? Am I phobic about the countryside or about my country? Nature or nationalism?

I remember a school trip to the Imperial War Museum and seeing a recruiting poster from 1915 of a young soldier astride a landscape painting. Above rolling green hills and partitioning hedgerows were the words *Your Country's Call.* At the bottom the question: *Isn't this worth fighting for?*

Nature, it seemed, was as much about propaganda as poetry.

'For me England is the country and the country is England,' said Prime Minister Stanley Baldwin in 1924. 'England comes to me from my various senses – through the ear, through the eye and through various imperishable scents.'

In 1733 the Scottish physician George Cheyne characterised nervousness as a disease of commercial prosperity and social progress. He called it 'the English Malady'. Cheyne's book argued that rich cuisine, artificial lighting, sedentary lifestyles, intemperance, urban living and avaricious greed had all conspired to make us sick: 'Since our Wealth has increas'd and our Navigation has been extended, we have ransack'd all the Parts of the Globe to bring together its whole Stock of Materials for Riot, Luxury, and to provoke Excess.'

On Agoraphobia

Nervousness, then, was a gilded cage, a response to the colonial project.

There is a politics to agoraphobia, as there is with everything else. A politics without an obvious political solution. I imagine the agoraphobic delegation on Mad Pride parades, our banners demanding . . . what exactly?

'Deep Breaths Now', 'Slow Down', 'Please, Take Me Home'.

In order to reclaim the streets we must first be able to leave the house.

I joke that my phobia votes Conservative. What it desires isn't revolution but a rule book.

Fear, like history, repeats itself. The first time as panic, the second as phobia. Marx's formula only adds to my neurotic script.

Agoraphobia is neither tragedy nor farce. It hovers between the two, reducible to neither, an occasion for both.

'We see agoraphobia as a paradigm for the historical intimidation and oppression of women', wrote Robert Seidenberg and Karen DeCrow in *Women Who Marry Houses*. 'The self-hate, self-limitation, self-abnegation and self-punishment of agoraphobia is a caricature of centuries of childhood instructions to women . . . Agoraphobics may well be the most completely uncompromising feminists of our time . . . Sensing that they are not welcome in the outside world, they have come to terms with their own sense of pride by not setting foot on land that is deemed alien and hostile.'

The most uncompromising feminists of our time? Would that my neurosis were such a bold act of radical defiance. Agoraphobia stems not from pride but from shame. It is a refusal unable to articulate what is being refused, more absurdist drama than agitprop.

Invisibility is the point, not the problem. The problem that *is* the point.

And (dare I ask) what about the male agoraphobic?

If I was proud of being agoraphobic I might be cured of it.

And then what would happen?

Incubation

'I can't name it. I only know I'm exposed.'

Henry James, _The Beast in the Jungle_

I am back at Warwick. I will soon be twenty years old. Weeks have gone by since that episode on the motorway. I appear to be asymptomatic. Life is lectures, life is the library. I lose myself in work, films, drunken nights in the union bar. Yet the panic attack has changed me, left an imprint as indelible as a birth mark.

I am in the bigger world I always thought I wanted. It is bigger – much bigger – than I ever imagined. My peers have long and complicated backstories: transnational, born, raised and schooled all in different places, places I know only through novels. Their food, like their dress sense, is elegant and foreign-sounding: aubergine, pomegranate, ratatouille. They take their freedom casually, are at ease with frontiers.

I seem to have reasons not to go anywhere: money, work. Reasons are never difficult to find, so long as they are never the actual reason. Agoraphobia is a fear that dare not speak its name.

'How could I have let such a thing slip past me?' The question from Anne Tyler's *Celestial Navigations*, a character asking it of her agoraphobic brother. 'Because Jeremy never stated it outright as a principle, that's why. He gave individual excuses, never the same one twice, whenever we invited him to someplace. To the park, to take fresh air.'

The agoraphobe is someone with a permanent alibi.

I should take another coach journey, prove to myself the earlier attack was a one-off. I don't do that. I turn down lifts to London, Birmingham, refuse offers of days out until people no longer ask. I berate myself for lack of courage. An inner monologue of self-recrimination. Which means my asymptomatic days are not asymptomatic at all.

I have another panic attack. Then another. Soon they become a daily fixture. In the supermarket, shopping precinct, on the bus into town. My nervous system moves to permanent high alert, ready for battle. Fear becomes familiar, expected. My unnormal normal.

On Agoraphobia

I read Angela Carter. *Nights at the Circus* has just been published. Whole paragraphs jump off the page. 'As soon as I'm out of sight of the abodes of humanity, my heart gives way beneath me like rotten floorboards,' says Fevvers, the novel's heroine. 'Nowhere, one of those words, like nothing, that opens itself inside you like a void. And were we not progressing through the vastness of nothing to the extremities of nowhere?'

The extremities of nowhere. Panic attacks do not lead to agoraphobia. The fear of them recurring does. Agoraphobia is a meta-fear, a pre-emptive strike against the fear yet to come. It is so frightened of fear that it insists you remain permanently afraid.

I develop a new game. I cannot stop playing it. It is called *What If?*

What if the panic happens again, somewhere where there is no escape? Motorways, open roads. No houses, no barns, no shelter. *What if* is a never-ending question. *Anticipatory anxiety*, the textbooks call it.

A record stuck in its groove.

Uninterrupted mental agony. Such were Ford Madox Ford's words about his phobic years. 'The illness was purely imaginary; that made it none the better . . . I wandered from nerve cure to nerve cure, all over England, Germany, Austria, Switzerland and Belgium.'

His list of countries makes me jealous, provokes the bitter question: just how agoraphobic were you? (Neurosis is rarely a site of solidarity.) Ford was that peculiar thing: a nomadic agoraphobe. Proof of the condition's capriciousness, the length of its reach.

Ford saw nineteen specialists, most of whom diagnosed sexual disorders. He endured cures ranging from enforced rest to ninety cold baths and thirty tepid soda-water douches in thirty days: 'I was so weak that even if the so-called agoraphobia had not interfered with my walking I should hardly have been able to get about.'

In 1904 the writer Olive Garnett recorded in her journal a visit she had made to see Ford: 'For a few days all went well; but it was a hot July, & on leaving Lake House . . . to walk over the Plain to Amesbury, Ford had an attack of agoraphobia, & said if I didn't take his arm he would fall down. I held on in all the blaze for miles, it seemed to me, but the town reached, he walked off briskly to get tobacco and a shave; and when I pointed this out to Elsie (Ford's wife) she said *nerves. He can't cross wide open spaces.*'

Jelly

'The nature of the medium through which the mind
acts and is acted upon, in sensation and voluntary
action, has . . . been a subject of much speculation.'

John Cooke, *A Treatise on Nervous Diseases* (1823)

Over the years the following diagnoses have been offered to
me by the medical profession: vestibular neuritis, temporal-
lobe epilepsy, labyrinthitis, vertigo, disturbed heart valve,
post-traumatic stress disorder, Ménière's disease, acoustic
neuroma, motion sickness and migraine. As I write this I hear
the words of Chekov, that wise doctor-writer: *The greater the
number of diagnoses, the more incurable the ailment.*

I have yet to encounter the model of the agoraphobic personality, although I am sure such a model exists. I imagine
a picture of a brain scan, a line of angry red dots all flashing
around the pre-frontal cortex and the words *thanks to devel-
opments in neuro-science we now know that . . .*

'Neuro' has become our new God-word, something that once spoken needs nothing more to be said.

Who knows? It may even turn out to be true.

In 1898 a doctor named J. H. Neale wrote in the journal the *Lancet*: 'I have referred to the possibility of recognising the agoraphobic as he walks along the street. Apart from the coarser evidence of his suddenly pausing to lay hold of a paling or to place a hand upon a wall, he will hardly ever be without a stick or umbrella, which you will notice he will plant at each step at some distance from him, in order to increase his line of support.'

Neale could easily have been describing my support group. When we meet we are invariably laden with props: walking sticks, headphones, gloves, caps, sunglasses, bags. We seem incomplete without them. Props stabilise our instability, are intimate and self-defining.

Unable to trust our perceptions, we turn to objects instead.

The group has over twenty members, although we barely reach double figures at any one meeting. Our youngest is in her early twenties, our oldest her mid-eighties. Two-thirds are women, all of us white. (Extremely white, complexions the colour of putty.) People get dropped off in cars, an occasional taxi. We are all nervous passengers.

Getting there *is* the therapy.

There is the middle-aged man, pot-bellied and goateed. He worked as a security guard in a shopping mall. He says he is trained to look for anything suspicious, but after a while everybody and everything looks suspicious. His job started to make him dizzy, gave him headaches.

He no longer goes to work, feels faint at the thought of shopping precincts, shops in general. He says, *There are too many fucking people.*

We have an elderly lady who talks about the fall she had one Christmas, how it robbed her of all confidence.

And the young girl who got beaten up in the city centre.

And the executive-looking man who had a car crash.

There is the grandmother who is convinced her children left the country *on purpose*, to spite her, to stop her from seeing the grandkids. It was, she tells us, deliberate. She will never forgive them.

There is the woman who always keeps her coat on, as though she is ready to leave at any moment. She has trouble picking her child up from school, gets anxious hours before; worrying, breathless. She thinks all the other parents are talking about her, judging her. She had always wanted to be a mother, was late becoming one. But now she isn't sure if she's any good at it. She says, *I've forgotten who I am*.

And there is a me, a fifty-something-year-old man with round glasses and a paperback permanently in his jacket pocket. He says he has a pathological fear of wide roads and open spaces, the problem being that anywhere can seem wide, everywhere can feel open.

We call it *checking in* as though we were at a hotel or an airport.

We trade one-liners:

Agoraphobia, the more I practise the worse it gets.

Agoraphobia, don't leave home without it.

Our coping strategies are varied and ingenious. They include: buying a dog, using a wheelchair, wearing ear muffs. We all carry medication, are portable chemists, rattling as we walk.

On Agoraphobia

We agree on trains being the least terror-inducing way to travel. It is something about the proximity of toilets and the presence of guards. The luminous lemon of their high-visibility jackets.

Agoraphobia is a fundamentalist form of belief. If it was a religion I would be scared of it. Agoraphobes are zealots, crazed clairvoyants: we *can* predict the future. Terrifying things will happen when we go out, because terrifying things always happen when we go out. Just wait and see.

I think of the mythic Cassandra, daughter of Priam, whose curse was an ability to predict terrible events that no one would believe. Like the agoraphobic, she was the victim of her own precognition.

'The phobia', writes Adam Phillips in *On Kissing, Tickling and Being Bored*, 'can be the one place in a person's life where meaning apparently never changes; but this depends upon one's never knowing what the meaning is.'

I'd love to but I can't. Our phobia is our most efficient – perhaps our only – bargaining tool. We get what we need by pathologising what we want.

Agoraphobia is a promissory note; it guarantees the future.

It can mean no more trips to the in-laws, or a way of staying close to the children. It ensures partners will be home on time, or that they will never leave us (will they?). It means certainty within its own prescribed realm of deep fearful uncertainty. It is our touchstone, our baseline, our absolute. Agoraphobia keeps us sane.

Support group members of all ages have embraced the New Age. Men with tattoos talk of meridians and dietary restrictions; respectably married women discuss their colons. We recommend Indian head massage, reflexology, vitamin cocktails, herbs, oils, reiki, acupuncture, floatation tanks, hypnotherapy, psychotherapy, aromatherapy, homeopathy. Over the years I have been a short-lived convert to all of them.

I am both infinitely sceptical and eternally hopeful.

There is, of course, a Facebook group. Many of them swear it has saved their lives, others flinch at its very mention, refer to it as the f-word.

I am a social-media agnostic. I have decided I will tackle cyberspace once I've mastered actual space, though I am aware such distinctions no longer apply.

On Agoraphobia

We lend each other books and return them (I suspect) unread. *Self-Help For Your Nerves, Living With Fear, Feel the Fear and Do It Anyway.*

'Put signs in your home that say, "So what? I'll handle it!"' advises the last of these. 'It is reported that over 90% of what we worry about never happens. That means that our negative worries have less than a 10% chance of being correct. If this is so, isn't being positive more realistic than being negative?'

I read the book and wonder what it means by the word *realistic.*

Yet I cannot stop reading them, even as I rail against their platitudes, about how they simply *don't get it.*

Or is that why I read them? Proof that my phobia – my most sacred fear – is something that cannot be got. Simply or otherwise.

There are echoes of the nineteenth century in these books, an immersion into a cold bath of progress and pragmatism. For William James – brother of Henry – this thing that went by 'the rather absurd name of agoraphobia' was an evolutionary throwback. James seemed offended by the persistence of such irrational fears, wondering if they had their roots in a redundant animality: 'Usually he slinks round the sides of the square, hugging the houses as closely as he can. This emotion has no utility in a civilised man but when we notice the chronic agoraphobia of our domestic cats, and see the tenacious way in which many wild animals, especially rodents, cling to cover . . . we are strongly tempted to ask whether such an odd kind of fear in us be not due to the accidental resurrection, through disease, of a sort of instinct which may in some of our ancestors have had a permanent and on the whole useful part to play?'

No utility in a civilised man, a phrase I have elevated to an in-joke with my latest shrink.

At the last count I have seen: ten psychiatrists, a score of counsellors, two dozen therapists. It's like a phobic version of the twelve days of Christmas. I can count them as others count sheep. I recall the knowing nods, the *so what you're telling me*s and the *and how did that make you feel*s. I ascribe them names, Dr Egelhoffer (from *His Girl Friday*), Doc Daneeka (from *Catch-22*), Dr Hannibal Lecter. They are the referees of my shrink CV, so much more impressive than my actual CV. Certainly longer.

On a scale of 0–10 with 0 being 'not at all' and 10 being 'the absolute worst'. The familiar litany of the questionnaire's questions, the prelude to CBT. Cognitive behavioural therapy is our new go-to place, a pill-free Prozac. Airlines offer it for fearful flyers, dentists to their patients, job centres to the unemployed.

CBT challenges what it calls *negative thinking*. Its practitioners tell me it does not matter why I have the issue, the important thing is to re-frame it, approach it like any other practical problem. They say things like *toxic* and *challenges* and use *evidence* as a verb.

We sit and categorise, itemise. I feel my fear flex its muscles.

And yet part of me knows it could be so much easier than this. Really. If I could only just . . . Stand up and stretch, stride purposefully down the gravel path and hitchhike a ride to . . . who knows where?

And who does know where? The question that endlessly baffles me. Given they can go anywhere, how do non-agoraphobic people decide where to go?

I vary my numbers – 7, 8, 9 – reluctant to give anything a melodramatic 10. Earnest young men and women ask me what proof I have for my beliefs, to follow them through to their nonsensical conclusions. Thus, goes the thinking, will the irrationality of my neurosis be laid bare. As though agoraphobia does not have a rationality of its own. Or being *laid bare* was not the problem to begin with.

If pushed, my hierarchy of fear reads something like this.

Non-negotiable: motorways, dual carriageways, unknown open roads.

Difficult: airports, shopping centres, busy main roads.

Variable: canals, parks, supermarkets.

Each item comes with its own footnote, its get-out clauses. The deck is constantly shuffled.

Shrink

'Fear of lightning, or fear of responsibility, of open places or of closed places, fear of society, fear of being alone, fear of fears, fear of contamination, fear of everything.'

George M. Beard, *American Nervousness* (1881)

By the end of the nineteenth century a whole new lexicon had emerged 'to describe the agoraphobic condition: 'Platzfurcht', 'peur des espaces', 'horreur du vide', 'topophobia', 'Platzangst', 'angoisse des places'.

In her book *Pathologies of Modern Space*, Kathryn Milun documents its various aetiologies: 'Agoraphobia was thought to be a problem of the liver (Cherchevsky) or the ear (M. Lannois and C. Tournier) . . . Insufficient will (Paul-Emil Levy) . . . excessive sex and alcohol (Henry Sutherland) or coffee (Legrand du Salle) . . . fatigue (Emil Cordes), childbearing (C. W. Suckling) . . . [a] species of epilepsy, an optical malfunction (M. Benedikt) . . . a degenerative nerve disease linked to syphilis (J. de Busscher).'

Key to this network of competing diagnoses was the work of one of Berlin's most distinguished neuroanatomists. Karl Friedrich Otto Westphal's previous research had included knee-jerk reflex, syphilis and obsessional mental states. On a trip to England he had studied reforms taking place in asylums and became an advocate for the removal of physical restraints on mental patients. In 1871, in a Prussian psychiatric journal, he published 'Die Agoraphobie, Eine Neuropathische Erscheinung'. Agoraphobia, A Neuropathic Phenomenon.

'A quiet, unpretending little man', is how George Eliot described him, meeting him on a trip to Berlin. A 'hideous branch of practice' is how she described his research, adding: 'I speak with all reverence: the world can't do without hideous studies.'

Westphal described three male patients: a thirty-two-year-old commercial traveller, a twenty-four-year-old merchant and a twenty-six-year-old engineer. Later he would treat a priest who could only leave the house under an umbrella, its shape reminding him of the roof of his parish church. And a soldier whose agoraphobia seemed to disappear when he dressed in his uniform: 'They all felt a peculiar uneasiness or anguish in crossing over wide squares or free, unenclosed spaces,' wrote Westphal.

Westphal's training can be heard in his inventory of one patient's features: 'Both eye sockets of the cranium show no dissimilarity, whereas the left eyebrow is somewhat lower . . . The left side of the face is smaller than the right side; the left ear is also longer . . . Both sides of the tongue are similar . . . The right hand is about ½ inch wider than the left one . . . The right shoulder is strong and a bit lower . . . The left part of the thorax is flatter but wider . . .' And on it goes. Physiological symmetry seems to be the key to psychic balance.

He does not consider 'a moderate degree of masturbation' to be relevant.

Electrical currents are tried to no avail. Pharmacological cures include: bromide of potassium, nervine tonics, valeriate of zinc, iron, quinine, phosphorous, cod-liver oil and stimulants. He writes of one patient whose self-cure is to make the acquaintance of a lady of the evening and walk along with her until safely home.

Westphal helped usher a new language into being, a science of morbid fear. 'The enumeration of phobias of all kinds became an almost obsessive part of clinical practice around the turn of the century', writes Anthony Vidler in *Warped Space*: 'Agoraphobia and its cognates emerged as commonplaces of conversation and lay diagnosis.'

It was competitive in its precision. Stasophobia (fear of elevated stations), cremnophobia (fear of precipices), lyssophobia (fear of liquids), oicophobia (returning home), monophobia (solitude), pyrophobia (fire), anthropophobia (social contact), triskaidekaphobia (the number 13).

In 1879 Benjamin Ball wrote to the Société Médico-Psychologique to report on his treatment of patients whose experience of panic in closed spaces he called 'claustrophobia', a condition that may appear to be the opposite of agoraphobia but which has in common a morbid dread associated with space.

The agoraphobe became a distinct category of person: named, identified, regulated. He (nearly all *he* at this point) took his place alongside those other inventions of the nineteenth century: the hypochondriac, the kleptomaniac, the neurasthenic.

In 1889 the architect Camillo Sitte remarked that agoraphobia was 'the universal trend of our time'.

On Agoraphobia

He joked that even statues may be at risk from this 'fashionable agoraphobia'.

For fashionable read *feminine*. And for feminine read *middle-class women or above*. The cooks, cleaners, scullery and chamber maids, the nurses and wet-nurses, the dressmakers and shop girls and the scores of other jobs done by working-class women were not seen as part of fashionable society, even though they made possible its every occasion. *Fashionable diseases* was shorthand for the litany of distress and eruption that was the bourgeois female body: vapours, flushes, dizziness, discomfort, fainting fits, headaches, delicate constitutions, backaches, constipation, pelvic disorders, irregular menstrua.

That such bodies had to be carried with modesty, beauty, virtue, elegance, moral superiority, fine wit, delicacy of feeling and irreproachable respectability goes without saying.

'A model of ladylike deportment and hyperfemininity,' writes Elaine Showalter in *The Female Malady*, describing ideals of nineteenth-century womanhood: 'a paradigm of that wasting beauty that the late Victorians found so compelling.'

There was a suspicion that such illnesses were part of a more nefarious strategy. The author of *Woman and Her Diseases* (1857) warned physicians to be aware of 'pretend hysteric attacks calculated to move our sympathy . . . and obtain some desired end.'

Vulnerability was allied to deceit, passivity a form of manipulation.

Agoraphobia began life as a story about men, written by men. Men in crisis. Somehow it ended up being a story about women. This should not perhaps be surprising, except for the fact that it is. Of the twenty-nine patients Westphal and his colleagues presented, only one of them was a woman.

In order to become fearful about public space, it is first necessary to have access to it. In this sense, agoraphobia was a condition of privilege, a privilege experienced as its exact opposite. It was a dramatic response to a situation that had otherwise been taken for granted. Public space was male space; space largely denied to women. People do not develop phobias about situations they have never known.

Permanently accompanied, cloistered, suffocatingly confined to the domestic sphere, how would the middle-class woman know if she was agoraphobic or not?

In her study of women in urban life – *The Sphinx in the City* – Elizabeth Wilson argues for urbanisation as being key to the origins of female emancipation. 'There were women as well as men in the urban crowd. Indeed the crowd was increasingly invested with female characteristics . . . The city, a place of growing threat and paranoia to men, might be a place of liberation for women. The city offers women freedom . . . It is *feminine* in its enclosing embrace, in its indeterminacy and labyrinthine uncenteredness.'

In its re-shaping of gender, the city brought agoraphobia a new constituency.

Men were feminised through nervous illness, and women were ill because they were women. Either way gender was agoraphobia's touchstone. Both Miss Havisham and Mr Fairlie's seclusions were rendered in terms of a gendered grotesque: the first as monstrous spinster, the second as foppish aesthete.

Collins and Dickens were writing for a Victorian England in which gender was being rapidly reconfigured to meet the changing nature of both empire and industry – a world in which manliness would move closer to Godliness. Perhaps even replace it.

During their lifetime physical education would become compulsory in the public schools, trickling down to produce a belief in the benefits of spectator sports, athletic clubs and Boys' Brigades. Neurotic interiority had no place in this athletic ideal.

In the first volume of *Parade's End*, Ford Madox Ford's Great War quartet, his hero goes walking with a woman in the countryside. He sees himself as a man whose heart belongs to a bygone age, one who prides himself on a code of honour. Christopher Tietjens is a married man; Valentine Wannop is not his wife. She is a new breed of woman: daring, single, a champion of a thing called 'women's suffrage'. Tietjens isn't sure what he thinks of his companion. Part of him disapproves of her, another part is beguiled. They come to a stile with an empty road beyond. The next stile is fifty yards away. Tietjens begins to panic, he starts to run: I hate roads where there are field paths, he says to her.

That's a phobia, like any woman's, she replies.

Gone Viral

'Still, if it was an exile, it was, for most of us,
exile in one's own home.'

Albert Camus, *The Plague*

My support group now meets via Zoom. Same day, same
time: everyone is agreed on the importance of maintaining
structure. We materialise like actors in a TV mini-series, the
screen rendering familiar faces unfamiliar. The ex-security
guard has shaved off his goatee. The woman who never takes
off her coat has taken off her coat. Her image flickers, keeps
cutting out.

We hurry through our weekly check-in, voices tech-
distorted, anxious to talk about what everybody is talking
about.

One woman says, *I don't see people, I see Petri dishes.* Another can barely contain her embittered satisfaction. She says, *I watch the news and think: Welcome to my world.*

This virus is supposed to be changing everything. But the much-touted 'new normal' isn't new to us.

'Stay at home and away from others.' So read the guidelines, instructions like a parody of Buddhist koans. It is a practice this group has been following for years. Agoraphobics are never short of reasons to stay indoors. Now we have hit the jackpot. Infections doubling every three days. The government's daily message switching tones: *Stay At Home* – from plea to instruction to threat.

It should be music to our ears. For once we are in vogue, ahead of the socio-medical curve. Most people with mental-health issues have spent lifetimes being told by medical professionals how important it is for us to leave the house. Now those same professionals are telling us how important it is for us not to. Should we not be dancing in the proverbial streets? Those streets we have spent years avoiding. On which we are no longer allowed to set foot.

Alongside compulsive handwashers, the spatial neurotic's moment has arrived. Agoraphobia is now government policy.

Sufferers of anxiety spend their time catastrophising the future. And so when an actual catastrophe arrives it can come as something of a relief. Our much anticipated worst case scenario has finally arrived; we call it everyday life. So *this* is what it feels like, the actual fear rather than a fantasy of it. The very worst *has happened*. Our dread is vindicated, rubber-stamped.

And it is not as dreadful as we imagined. Because nothing could be. The anxious imagination outstrips reality at every turn.

Self-isolating it is being called, as though mere *isolation* were not weighty enough. The phrase sounds crushingly contemporary but can be traced back to (at least) 1873 and Wilkie Collins' *No Name*, a novel centred around disguise and dubious legitimacy.

The book contains another of his grotesques – Mrs Wragge, a half-witted giant married to a duplicitous captain. Whenever he verbally attacks her, Collins asks: 'Was she still self-isolated from her husband's deluge of words? Perfectly self-isolated.'

Self-isolation: refuge, then, as well as quarantine.

A fear of going out is different from a law against doing so, but the two can form an unstable coalition. Both my neurosis and my government insist I stay at home. They agree it is the best way to keep me safe. I am moving from *cannot* to *must not*, my phobia blurring into state-sanctioned prohibition.

Please mind the gap. Thus do London's Tubes remind their customers to be spatially aware. The advice now sounds eerily quaint, a steampunk throwback to a world still discovering far-fetched concepts like Health and Safety. And when such things were still viewed with suspicion, the punchline to tabloid outrage.

Mind the gap – as evident between generations as it is between the customers queuing outside Sainsbury's. Hands up who knew how long two metres was. Now put them down if you are over fifty. In the course of four weeks I have become a metric convert. I calculate the distance between myself and other people via an imaginary index of nasal emissions and mucal spray. We look at each other and apologise with our eyes: the only thing visible above scarves or medical masks.

On Agoraphobia

The collective fear is cancelling out more specific fears. The supermarket was one of my most pronounced phobic sites. Its crowds and congested aisles used to make me hyperventilate, drop my basket and run. Now it feels welcoming, a place of solidarity. One in one out, security guards and orderly queues, the once unmanageable chaos of shopping finally feels managed, held.

Stay At Home. How you hear this instruction depends on the kind of home you have. Emma has moved in. We can't be the only ones being forced to road test their new relationship. A new genre may emerge – accidental co-habitation – the dystopian rom-com.

We are inoculating ourselves with books, looking to narrative for tentative reassurance. We seem to be drawn to reading about the experience of war: Olivia Manning's *Fortunes of War*, Pat Barker's *Regeneration* novels, Jane Gardham's *Old Filth*. It is an obvious enough reference point, although I suspect the fact they are all trilogies is just as important. One book holds out the promise of the next, giving shape and sequence to an experience that has neither.

I wonder where the peddlers of religious apocalypse have gone. Like every other trader they have been banished from the high street. There was one particular man who used to stand in Nottingham's Market Square near where I live.

Occasionally I would stop and chat to him, ask him how he could be so certain of his predictions. He told me he had repented, accepted Jesus Christ as his saviour. I imagine him now tucked up in his bedroom, surveying his supplies of tinned food, a maniacal prophet delighting in the torments of the damned.

Not that I feel like the damned (but maybe the damned never do). If you had asked me a month ago to imagine a world without cinemas, theatres or libraries, I would have said it sounded like a vision of hell, the setting of a post-apocalyptic movie. Yet apocalypse is precisely what this is not. It is closer to entropy – the random energy produced by molecular disorder. It is empty trams as well as full-to-bursting hospitals.

Every Thursday night at 8 pm the doorstep applause, erupting like a three-minute punk track, cacophonous and uncannily crisp. I imagine the noise recorded by Steve Reich or Philip Glass, a minimalist fanfare, a soundtrack both oceanic and impersonal.

I take my one walk per day, stride briskly around the local park. I have had my share of therapy here, stood with clinical psychologists armed with bio-feedback machines and betablockers as I tried to control the mounting panic. The aim was to desensitise my nervous system, re-program the cognitive associations between empty space and fear. The focus was on breathing, a steady heartbeat, teaching the so-called sympathetic nervous system that it had no reason for either *flight* or *fight*. The psychologist used to say I should come here daily, that repeated exposure would eventually produce a phobia-free response.

He would say, *You will get there eventually. There really is nothing to be frightened of.*

Bright Red

'In trying to grasp ourselves, we clutch,
shuddering, at nothing.'

Theodor Adorno, *Minima Moralia*

It is my second year at Warwick. I am twenty years old. The university is experiencing the final throes of student radicalism: miners' strike, Greenham Common, the growing threat of AIDS. Our badges all have acronyms, our T-shirts slogans. Student politics is still a viable career, just. We throw eggs at the Home Secretary, boycott South African goods, learn to replace *girl-* or *boyfriend* with *partner*.

We are the last generation to receive grants.

Two grand a year to mis-pronounce Derrida.

And Barthes and Foucault and Kristeva, the trinity of French theory without whom no undergraduate essay felt complete.

On Agoraphobia

They allowed us to swagger, these critics who wrote like poets. They were dense and alluring, seductively aphoristic. Their sentences made me swoon. *Language is a skin: I rub my language against the other.* Thus did I discover a new mode of being, one that began with *the word.* 'These body fluids,' wrote Julia Kristeva in *Powers of Horror*, 'this defilement, this shit are what life withstands, hardly and with difficulty, on the part of death. There, I am at the border of my condition as a living being.'

I read her and gasp, forced to stand up from the chair in which I sit reading. I did not know it was possible to do *this*. Like the Catholic theology I had abandoned, the spell was in the enigma. It was proof of revelation. Nothing this strange could be anything other than true.

This language belonged not just to the library, but could be found in the weekly dispatches of the music press. *The Face*, *New Musical Express* and *Melody Maker* were not just papers about music. For a certain kind of reader, they were an arts school education, a how-to manual, a Situationist manifesto. Their writers had absorbed all that elegiac theory and allied it to writing about contemporary popular culture. It produced some of the most vital prose of its time, written by journalists as experimental and elliptical as the musicians and filmmakers they were writing about.

And their pages were open to anyone. Even agoraphobic young men at red-brick universities. I buy an Olivetti typewriter.

My fear of travel spreads, like ink poured into a fish tank. The very thought of leaving campus turns my blood to ice. Outside I seek visual markers, guarantors of safety: garden beds, ice-cream van, flower stall, one person (but no more) walking ahead of me, stationary cars, a clock tower.

I take detours: avoid bridges, parks, open ground. I am the road less travelled.

I read R. D. Laing until the spine breaks, the pages of *The Divided Self* jutting out like a badly shuffled deck of cards. I quote his maxims to myself as though they were prayers: 'Insanity – a perfectly rational adjustment to an insane world.' 'Madness need not be all breakdown. It may also be break-through.' 'Life is a sexually transmitted disease and the mortality rate is one hundred per cent.'

Laing had caught the 1960s moment and it was still resonating twenty years later. Anti-psychiatry was a cornerstone of the counter-culture, part of a wider challenge to a world that equated cure with normalcy.

On Agoraphobia

In 1966 – the year after Laing published *The Divided Self* – an article appeared in the *British Journal of Psychiatry*. It was entitled 'Modified Leucotomy in Severe Agoraphobia: A Controlled and Serial Inquiry' and reported the outcomes of prefrontal lobotomies performed on twenty-two agoraphobic patients (four male, eighteen female).

'In patients with much general anxiety, desensitization becomes a Sisyphean task because of the repeated regeneration of phobias. In the present series, as soon as leucotomy (lobotomy) had reduced anxiety this obstacle was removed, and desensitization could then be applied usefully . . . These findings indicate that the leucotomy operation should be part of a wider treatment programme. Once anxiety falls after operation, patients should be retrained to go out.'

Cut a chunk out of the brain and the mind will follow.

A Sisyphean task: the mythological figure condemned by the gods to spend eternity pushing a huge rock uphill only to have it tumble down again. The reference here raises an interesting question: who exactly is Sisyphus, the agoraphobics or the psychiatrists whose job it was to treat them?

Reflecting on Sisyphus, Albert Camus once wrote: 'The struggle itself towards the heights is enough to fill a man's heart. One must imagine Sisyphus happy.'

Such existential stoicism was not a position shared by the editorial board of the *British Journal of Psychiatry*. Comparing its control to its trial group the report concluded: 'It must be noted, however, that no patient in either series did highly skilled work; leucotomy might have impaired this more. For relatively undemanding occupations, however, the amount of personality change produced by leucotomy with these operations was not usually excessive.'

(*Undemanding occupations*: the name of another novel I will never write.)

As late as 1974 the editors of the *British Medical Journal* would review the available treatment for agoraphobia and report: 'There is also evidence that psycho-surgery may be beneficial. A retrospectively controlled trial showed benefit from lower medial quadrant leucotomy.'

Decades later and Laing has been superseded by Foucault. I carry his *Madness and Civilisation* around with me. Occasionally I even read it. Foucault awakens me to an

83

emancipatory despair. Psychiatry was just another means of social control, a way of policing dissent or, more corrosive still, getting the dissenters to police themselves. The 'insane' had simply internalised society's faultlines, introjected the chaos at the heart of capitalism.

I acquire the requisite student wardrobe: Oxfam jackets, T-shirts, skinny black jeans, Dr Marten shoes. The jackets are too big; clothes to hide in, disguise rather than display. I drown in the cavernous folds of my overcoat. Shirts are black, white, plaid: they aspire to anonymity. I wear sunglasses regardless of the weather.

On the doorstep of the halls of residence is a launderette where I don't do my laundry. Next to it a burger bar, supermarket and bank. The bars sell subsidised lager. I live in an out-of-season holiday camp. Life exists within a fifty-yard radius.

It is easy to be agoraphobic if you never leave campus. And if you never leave campus it is easy to become agoraphobic. The university looms up out of nowhere, a mirage. Shimmery red buildings, grey concrete, cold, cold steel.

'The Outside World is a particularly meaningless phrase at Warwick,' wrote E. P. Thompson in Warwick University Limited in 1970, 'especially for those who live on the site in halls of residence . . . It is quite possible not to move from the campus for weeks.'

I am surrounded by arterial roads. The labyrinthine swirl of the overpass, the ring road disappearing into a vanishing point. Neither urban nor suburban, but inter-urban. *Edgelands* they would later be called by the psycho-geographers who explored them. Places that are un-places.

Coventry is the nearest city, the place George Eliot came to live when she was sixteen and still Mary Ann Evans. In *Daniel Deronda* she wrote of her heroine, Gwendolen Harleth: 'She was ashamed and frightened, as at what might happen again, in remembering her tremor in suddenly feeling herself alone, when, for example, she was walking without companionship and there came a rapid change in the light. Solitude in any wide scene impressed her with an undefined feeling of immeasurable existence aloof from her, in the midst of which she was helplessly incapable of asserting herself.'

Left

'It could well be just a lump in the throat, this globe.
In fact, you could cough it right up and spit it out.'

Olga Tokarczuk, *Flights*

At some point between the fourth and fifth centuries BC, Hippocrates, the founder of modern medicine, wrote of one who 'through bashfulness, suspicion, and timorousness will not be seen abroad, loves darkness as life and cannot endure the light or to sit in lightsome places; his hat still in his eyes, he will neither see, nor be seen by his good will. He dared not come in company for fear he should be misused, disgraced, overshoot himself in gesture or speeches, or be sick.'

We may no longer believe in Greco-Roman medicine, but we do believe in *temperament*. A legacy of the four humours: sanguine, choleric, melancholic, phlegmatic. Each would have been matched with their humoral fluid – blood, yellow bile, black bile and phlegm. A philosophy of seasons and elements, holistic in the truest sense of the word. The whole picture.

Loves darkness as life. It is a picture in which winter is the true state of affairs. The only season to feel natural. Summer is an aberration.

She lies cat-like in the garden, a lazy Sunday in September. She's soaking up the last days of summer, sighs as she tells me there's not many more left. I go inside and switch on the TV. The BBC are showing an old Cary Grant movie – *Penny Serenade*. Cary and Irene Dunn are wanting to adopt a child. It's not going to end well.

I look at her through the window, striped navy dress and brown sun hat. I wonder if our relationship to space is a question about intimacy, the ease (or otherwise) with which we hold our most private thoughts.

Emma realises herself outdoors in a way that remains alien to me. It is as though she emotionally expands, an inner calm finding its match in the breezy stillness.

There are people who *belong* outdoors, who use open space to gain access to themselves. I will never be – have never been – one of them. There are times when I think of my agoraphobia as a distillation of who I am, the very essence of me.

Inside is where I unfold myself, always has been, long before phobia raised its Janus-face. Rugs by the fireplace, a chair in the kitchen. The point of being outside is to look forward to coming back in.

Meet me in a cafe and I will be sat in a corner, my back to the wall. I will joke that the gunmen will never catch me unprepared.

The garden is not one of my phobic places, but in it I feel vaguely abandoned. I pluck grass, I fidget, I look for things to do. It seems there is always something needs re-arranging, fixing. Emma teases me, quotes her beloved Jane Austen: *It is not everyone who has your passion for dead leaves.*

There is a painting I once saw by the artist Ivon Hitchens. It was a dazzling splurge of 70s psychedelia, a raging mesh of mouthwash foam and cheap acid pink. It has been years since I saw it, but I can recall it as vividly as a family photograph. The image seemed larger than the canvas, it threatened to burst out of the edges of the frame. It was one bad, bad trip. The painting is simply called *Outside*.

In 1993 the artist Rachel Whiteread became the first woman to win the Turner Prize, with a sculpture she called *House* – the cast of the inside of an entire Victorian terraced house. She exhibited it at the site of the original dwelling in Mile End – Grove Road, a street in which all the other houses had been pulled down. It remains one of the starkest visual representations of the agoraphobic uncanny I have ever seen.

I am looking at a photograph of it now. It is a spatial full stop, an insoluble Rubik's cube, inviting meaning even as it repels it. There are doors you can't open, rooms you can't enter, a domestic space negating all domesticity. The inside has become the outside, no distinction between the two. I am reminded of that line from Ford and Conrad's *The Inheritors*: 'nothing within: no rooms, no hollow places.'

Our relationship to space is as fundamental as our relationship to our bodies. Scrub that. It *is* our relationship to our bodies. It is like our sexuality. As much biology as culture. Space is where our bodies end. And we are never quite sure where that might be.

At the 1997 *Sensation* exhibition, Whiteread exhibited *Untitled (One Hundred Spaces)*, a series of resin casts of the space underneath chairs. The sculptures looked like ice-cubes, solidified jellies. They were displayed again recently at Tate Britain. I walked around them on tiptoe. The desire to touch them, to taste them, was almost overwhelming.

Space reveals our appetites. Is this the source of my phobic shame, why it sometimes feels closer to a fetish than a neurosis?

I suspect that people who have witnessed me in full agoraphobic meltdown – the blind panic and desperate flights – know me in ways usually reserved only for lovers.

I am never quite able to forgive them their knowledge, their intimacy with my most personal unsafe space.

Safe space: a concept which, for the agoraphobe, verges on the oxymoronic. It's a phrase I hear almost daily now, particularly in spaces where safety is already assured: cinemas, art galleries, university seminars. Surely they don't come much safer than that?

I feel unsafe whenever someone says, *This is a safe space*. Always announced with such certainty, such sanctimonious conviction. It feels both premature and solicitous: a sensitivity to what we suppose other peoples' sensitivities might be. *This is a safe space*. How do you know this; what steps have been taken to ensure it? Am I being reassured or scrutinised? Saying a thing does not guarantee it. In fact it evokes the possibility of its opposite. *This is a safe space.* Really? Since when? For how long? How unsafe did it used to be?

Because we cannot police the unconscious. Offer as many trigger warnings as you want but memory will still find a way to wrong-foot you. The smell of aftershave on a tram, the way the man in the coffee shop adjusts his tie.

When shell-shocked soldiers returned from the trenches of the Great War, their trauma was not triggered by going to watch Charlie Chaplin films, or looking at the paintings of Otto Dix. They were triggered by cars backfiring, or the sound of a plate smashing on a kitchen floor. Anything could be a trigger.

And what might be a trigger one day could well be a source of comfort the next. We only know what our triggers are when they happen to us.

Maybe 'triggers' are what we reach for instead of 'moods', customised replacements for those much less malleable – less manageable – turns of the mind. The idea of a trigger implies logic, cause and effect. It soothes us, suggests we have identified the problem, if not solved it. We are in control. No need to worry.

On Agoraphobia

A mood, like a phobia, offers no such comforts. Dark, disconsolate, wretched, it is an affront to our image of ourselves.

Describing a phobia can often feel like recounting a dream – inescapably falsifying. You end up imposing a consistency – a rogue sequentiality – on an experience which has precisely neither.

It is no coincidence that the director whose films best dramatised phobia was also preoccupied with dreams. Hitchcock understood that both states provide the keys to our desires. *Spellbound*, *Marnie* and *Vertigo* are all films about the way neurotic states protect us from what we want. For Hitchcock phobia was frozen desire; a romance looking for ways to be thwarted.

In interviews Hitchcock used to tell the story of being sent aged five to the local police station by his father with a note. The policeman read the note and locked young Alfred up in a cell for a few minutes. Hitchcock would say the experience left him scared stiff of anything to do with the law. He would not even drive for fear of getting a parking ticket.

Law, parents, enclosure. Phobia's founding fathers.

Show

'What kind of camouflage is that which exists to make
one not invisible, but ever more distinct?'

Elfriede Jelinek, 'Sidelined'

For someone with a fear of exposure, writing a memoir may
seem a strange occupation: counter-intuitive, masochistic
even. If avoidance is my phobia's signature, why would I
invite it to take centre stage? And if my darkest fears are
the things about myself I least understand, what hope do a
few black marks on white paper have of solving it? Can *The
Autobiography of an Agoraphobic* be anything more than a
disappearing act?

Writing and agoraphobia: the links seem to me manifold, and
not just because I am afflicted by both. Blank spaces, infinite
possibilities, paralysing freedom. Writing discovers where it
wants to go by getting there. It demands you become your
own cartographer.

On Agoraphobia

To write about one's life is to conceal as well as reveal it, as much magic trick as intimate whisper. It is a trust exercise, a confidence game. Its disclosures are a way of protecting myself.

When it goes well I am struck by the thought *I got lucky*. Had I started writing two hours later, those words would not have come. Not in the order they did.

I can never fully shake off the suspicion that the page is not truly blank. Or not blank enough. It is haunted by the traces of everything I have ever read, the words I have yet to write.

Agoraphobia and writing. I imagine an anthology: *The Agoraphobic Reader: Selected Writings By and About* . . .

The book would contain Proust, Fernando Pessoa and Bolesław Prus. Kate Atkinson would rub shoulders with Philip K. Dick, Stef Penney with J. D. Salinger. There would be George Mackay Brown, Elfriede Jelinek and Penelope Gilliatt. There would be chapters on the differences between Reclusion and Seclusion, on Rural and Urban, on Exile and Prison.

And there would be a chapter on 'David' – subject of *The Autobiography of David*, published in 1946, long since out of print, assembled and transcribed by his friend the novelist Ernest Raymond.

Everyone who met David remarked on how good-looking he was, not just handsome but innocent and otherworldly. The poet Edwin Muir said he looked as though he spent his time listening to the angels.

He had been raised in Glasgow – one of seven children of God-fearing, teetotal Presbyterians.

His first attack came when he was a small child: 'I was trying to climb Ben Varren, and halfway up I was suddenly seized with what would now be called agoraphobia . . . The great, lonely granite boulders, the mighty, towering, precipitous ravines . . . produced in me a sense of immensity, a feeling of being lost, of being a minute particle without any habitation or place of rest in a menacing material universe which offered no means of coming into its heart.'

He joined the army but was discharged on account of his condition. He moved to Canada, where he lived as a vagabond, waiter, actor, sailor. He returned to the UK, regularly finding himself committed to various mental asylums.

On Agoraphobia

His treatment often consisted of orderlies dragging him across the neighbouring fields of the hospital. As he wryly comments, his agoraphobia meant escape was impossible.

David came to believe that his suffering had a wider purpose: 'I began to see the human race against the background of history – a tragic, yet a beautiful thing, toiling, praying, fighting, singing, up from the apes to primitive man, and now on to a dawning consciousness of immense undeveloped power; it was a unity. What I had suffered the race too had suffered.'

He worked as a graphologist – a respectable branch of fortune-telling, by his own account. He moved into journalism on Fleet Street, first freelance then as editor. He interviewed Ramsay MacDonald and rubbed shoulders with Bonar Law, Lord Rothermere, H. G. Wells, John Galsworthy, Winifred Holtby, the Stracheys, Arnold Bennett and George Bernard Shaw. He was a supporter of women's suffrage, a pacifist who set up the Arbitrate First Bureau – a group whose aim was to provide educational support for the League of Nations.

And through all this the fear. He secures interviews only to turn back when confronted by a space he cannot cross. He refuses invitations from editors to their places in the country. 'The outdoor disability – I could not go further than fifty yards from a house – prevented me from joining in any form of outdoor exercise, but, worst of all, it made friendship with men almost impossible . . . Men usually wanted to walk in the country; I could not go. Because of this I had a dread of summer, when social meetings were so often in the open . . . In taking stock of my position, I had to admit that life at the best was tremendously dangerous for me, a razor-edge business.'

David's story is an intriguing account of an agoraphobic – the portrait of a life whose day-to-day patterns are structured by fear. Yet something else bubbles beneath it – a subplot which may also be the actual plot.

The book is also a record of his struggle with a compulsion to sexual exhibitionism, what he calls his morbid impulse: 'For about a year I never went out of doors without the fear that I might expose myself. The acuteness of the agony that this cost me was probably greater than any of my other dreads . . . I saw myself as not only a nervous and physical wreck, but as a moral viper, an outcast unfit for the company of decent men and women. I found it always more difficult to overcome this fear if I had been through a difficult time with my other phobias, such as the dread of crossing certain streets or places, or the fear of sudden death.'

A fear of exposure; the erotics of exposure. Phobia and sexuality are the two things about ourselves which refuse to be contained. David hides one in the other, aware they share a common impulse. He succumbs on more than one occasion, is arrested, sent to other asylums. At one point he goes to a nudist colony in the hope that constant exposure to flesh will deaden its allure.

It doesn't.

He frets that the perversion and the phobia are related, is troubled by their unknowable correlation. They seem to be each other's cause, each other's relief. Hitchcock should have made a movie out of him. David was a Freudian ready-made if ever there was one.

Couch

'Inability to tolerate empty space limits
the amount of space available.'

Wilfred Bion, *Cogitations*

Freud never met David, although he might well have been describing him when he wrote: 'The agoraphobic patient imposes a restriction on [the] ego so as to escape a certain instinctual danger – namely, the danger of giving way to his erotic desires . . . I may cite as an instance the case of a young man who became agoraphobic because he was afraid of yielding to the solicitations of prostitutes . . . The phobia of being alone is unambiguous in its meaning: it is, ultimately, an endeavour to avoid the temptation to indulge in solitary masturbation.'

If, for the nineteenth century, agoraphobia was a symptom of modern urbanity, Freud's intervention was to re-describe it in terms of psychic displacement. He viewed the phobic scene – buildings, streets and plazas – as symbolic of repressed fears and desires. It is not the empty environment from which we recoil, but ourselves – or rather those parts of ourselves which lie buried, hidden, and which we transfer onto the objects and spaces around us. 'In the case of phobias one can see clearly how this internal danger is transformed into an external one,' he wrote: 'The agoraphobic is always afraid of his impulses in connection with temptations aroused in him by meeting people on the street . . . In his phobia he makes a displacement and is now afraid of an external situation.'

A phobia is a drama in which our unconscious gets brought to life.

There are theories that Freud himself was agoraphobic. In *The Search Within*, Theodor Reik, fellow analyst and disciple of Freud's, recalls walking with him in their native Vienna: 'We crossed a street that had heavy traffic, Freud hesitated as if he did not want to cross. I attributed the hesitancy to the caution of the old man, but to my astonishment he took my arm and said, "You see, there is a survival of my old agoraphobia, which troubled me much in younger years."'

Freud the agoraphobic. It's a tantalising admission; it does not feature prominently in our collective portrait of the man.

Does it discredit his readings of agoraphobia, or validate them?

It was in an essay of 1897 that Freud made his most controversial claim about the condition. 'Agoraphobia seems to depend on a romance of prostitution,' he wrote in 'The Architecture of Hysteria', 'a woman who will not go out by herself asserts her mother's unfaithfulness.'

Fear *of* the streets is a fear of the kind of woman she might become *on* the streets, the promise and the threat of her own sexuality.

Streets represent the opportunity for illicit encounters, for the woman to become the prostitute she both envies and fears. Streets produce street-walkers.

Freud's diagnosis may sound jarring today. Yet, for better or worse – for better *and* worse – his impact on our understanding of agoraphobia is with us still. We may no longer be Freudians but we accept that people have a past, and that their past stays with them. We believe in reasons, even when those reasons do not seem reasonable. Encounter an agoraphobe in fiction or film and we instantly suspect something about them, sense something is not right. A character's agoraphobia is always a prelude to their backstory. Freud made the agoraphobic into a dramatis persona, ensured that it is the sufferer herself to whom we should pay attention.

He had already treated three agoraphobics by 1897 – the time when he met a five-year old boy who was afraid to go out into the streets of Vienna. Little Hans (as he called him, real name Herbert Graf) had witnessed a horse falling and became fearful of leaving his house as a result.

Freud met Hans only once, leaving his father to supervise an analysis that was conducted mostly through corre-spondence. Hans talked about the horse's teeth and its harness (its 'moustache'). But what had truly alarmed him was the size of its penis – what he referred to as its 'widdler'.

Hans was three and three-quarter years old (Freud is at pains to be exact) when he made an important discovery: *A dog and a horse have widdlers; a table and chair haven't.*

'He had thus got hold of an essential characteristic for dif-ferentiating between animate and inanimate objects,' writes Freud. 'Thirst for knowledge seems to be inseparable from sexual curiosity.'

Hans becomes preoccupied by the question of the phallus, its size and provenance. He asks his father if he has one and why he has not seen it. He tells his mother, *I thought you were so big you'd have a widdler like a horse.* When his sister Hannah is born he does not at first like her, wonders why she has no teeth. After a week he notices that her widdler's still quite small . . . *When she grows up it'll get bigger all right.*

The phallus and sexual difference: the most contested area of sexual politics. The thing we have – or have not – that makes us who we are. The possession we never quite possess.

The phallus bestows the very status it confounds. It is the gift that keeps on giving. Except we are never quite sure what is being given. Or who has given it to us. Or when they will take it away.

Hans reported two key fantasies to his father, both of which the father reported to Freud. In the first there was a big giraffe and a crumpled one: *and the big one called out because I took the crumpled one away from it. Then it stopped calling out: and I sat down on the crumpled one.*

In the second a plumber came and removed his bottom and widdler, and then gave him another one of each, but larger.

Freud sounds delighted – triumphant – in his recounting of Hans' story. He finds in the five-year-old boy a re-enactment of the Oedipal conflict he was to make central to his work. Young boy sees father as rival, is symbolically castrated by him, is reconciled to becoming like him. It is a classic three-act structure, as old as Greek tragedy, as everyday as soap opera. We call it growing up, abandoning what we want to become the adults we have no choice but to be.

Horses, harnesses and widdlers: fathers, moustaches and incestuous desire. The case history of Little Hans seems folkloric now, so obviously Freudian, as it were.

How strange psychoanalysis must have sounded to the middle-class ears of fin-de-siècle Vienna. All that talk of widdlers and castration. All that intolerable desire. (What did Hans' parents tell the neighbours?)

Freud recalls in a postscript to the 1922 edition of Hans' story how he later met him on a railway journey: 'The publication of this first analysis of a child had caused great stir and even greater indignation, and a most evil future had been foretold for the poor little boy, because he had been "robbed of his innocence" at such a tender age and been made the victim of a psychoanalysis . . . None of these apprehensions had come true. Little Hans was now a strapping youth of nineteen. He declared that he was perfectly well, and suffered from no troubles or inhibitions.'

Graham Caveney

We haven't ignored Freud, we've popularised him – a much more effective way of closing someone down.

I have a daydream in which I meet Freud and tell him he is now mostly taught as a branch of literary and cultural theory, that his books are nowhere to be found on the shelves of a psychiatric profession for whom psychoanalysis is either empirically discredited or politically disreputable. I show him David Suchet and Montgomery Clift in the bio-pics, Peter Sellers in *What's New Pussycat?*. We watch Hitchcock's *Spellbound* together and he laughs when the nymphomaniac tells Ingrid Bergman that *psychoanalysis bores the pants off me*.

I tell him we have robbed the word *dreams* of its oneirism, its shocking surreality. Freud thought of them as *the royal road to the unconscious*, we think of them as fodder for the ad man, a tangible thing we can realise, fulfil, *be*.

Rather than telling us something surprising about ourselves, something unknown and unexpected, we have instead put dreams to work. We have made them a shorthand for aspirational lifestyles: beaches, sunsets, celebrity.

We are, we are told, living the dream. Which raises the question, what becomes of our actual dreams?

Hard Shoulder

'A fast-moving motorway is not a place for the
encouragement of interest in flowering shrubs.'

**Sir Eric Savill, Letter to the Landscape Advisory
Committee in 1958**

I cannot drive, have never driven. I come from a family
for whom driving was both unaffordable and unnecessary.
Descriptions of cars were limited to their colour and size,
their various makes a language to which we had no access.
When people told car jokes – gags about Skodas or Mini
Metros – there would be a pause whilst I tried to work out
the punchline from the context.

My parents walked to work, took the bus into town. Our
lives existed within a four-mile area.

A parked car still strikes me as an uncanny object. Unclear
as to whom they belong, it feels as though they never quite

belong anywhere. Private property abandoned in a public space, like a solitary glove at a bus stop, or soil on a carpet. Ghostly provenance.

I often want to nudge them, have to resist a spiteful dig of the elbow. I want to make them howl, hear the primal scream of their alarm.

It has been thirty-six years since I was last on a motorway, a near lifetime of compromise and embarrassed excuses. I try not to take a reckoning, avoid tormenting myself with the missed funerals, unattended weddings, jobs turned down.

(I cringe at other memories: the emergency phone calls, the A&E admissions.)

I once panicked on a motorway and so motorways make me panic. It is a classic behaviourist model, one to make Pavlov proud. I am offended by my own predictability.

At my most agoraphobic everywhere outside my front door can feel like that originary motorway. The birth of my phobia, its apotheosis.

The road was meant to be a symbol of freedom, the car the embodiment of a particular kind of future. There was a kid on our street who used to wolf-whistle every time he saw certain makes of car drive by: *Would you look at the body on that?* He talked about cars as though they were film stars, a source of pure libidinal fascination.

Like all true fetishists it was the language that moved him, the talk of cylinders and pistons and turbo compressors. It was not difficult to hear the subtext to his passion. Underneath all his fuel-injected fantasy lay a very simple statement: *Here is proof that my life might be different.*

My great-uncle Jimmy had helped build the motorways on which I am afraid to travel. He was just one of the thousands who left Ireland in the 1950s to work here as navvies. He had worked on the Preston Bypass (later part of the M6) and had been there on the 5th of December 1958, the day the Prime Minister, Harold Macmillan, opened it. Jimmy boasted that Lancashire's motorways were as solid and true as the Los Angeles freeways.

I adored Jimmy, his tall tales grew taller every time he told them. He was the one person we knew who owned a car. In the summer he would take us for days out to the seaside, or simply drive us to motorway service stations where we would sit on the bridge and watch the traffic flow by beneath us. Burtonwood, Charnock Richard, Forton: these places were more adventurous than the places to which we were travelling. They belonged to a science-fiction film: their toilets were metallic, their food fluorescent. I wanted to live in a motorway service station.

I am still in short pants, my leg stuck like chewing gum to the leather seat. In my lap a book – *I-Spy On the Motorway* – part of a series all purporting to be written by a 'Red Indian' – Big Chief I-Spy and his trusty sidekick Hawkeye. The book gives you points for spotting things – road signs, cattle, police cars. I look out the window at the signs. They are huge and bold, white on blue; the colour of nurses' uniforms.

The motorway ushered in an age of accelerated modernity. Along with the TV and transistor radio, the motorway signalled a further step in the post-war democratisation of Britain. The smoky grime of the railways was to be consigned to the museums, a relic of bygone Victoriana. The motorway would revolutionise work, bring commuter belts and New Towns.

If cars meant aspiration and mobility, then motorways would be the route to making those things real, would crystallise them in technicoloured tarmac.

A year after the Preston Bypass came the M1, seventy-four miles stretching from St Albans to Rugby. 'This motorway starts a new era in road travel,' said Ernest Marples, the new Minister of Transport. 'It is a powerful weapon to add to our transport system. But like all powerful instruments it can be a power for good or evil.'

In their early days British motorways were empty, with no speed limit or safety belts or crash barriers. Driving along the motorway was a day out in itself, an adventure. The country was one giant magic carpet.

I no longer play I-Spy on the motorway. I am an adult who clings to a diagnosis of agoraphobia because he does not know what else to call it. Motorways turn me into a book with the pages ripped out. They dissolve and refuse me. Suspend my body in frantic stasis.

Over Here

'The British feed themselves on our banality without
catching our excitement and gusto.
Many of them now chew gum.'

Edmund Wilson, *Europe Without Baedeker*

It is a weirdly specific amount (£7.38), payment for a three-hundred-word review: Ivor Cutler at the Warwick Arts Centre. I am twenty years old and can now call myself a published writer. The *NME* no less, the place that had once seemed as glamorous and out of reach as the Left Bank.

I look at my name in print. It is like catching a glimpse of myself in a shop window. I wonder what the relationship is between me and him. I decide I much prefer him.

Work breeds work. I get used to the sight of bulging jiffy bags secured with gaffer tape. Books for review. Advanced Proofs. There is something intimate about them. They say:

On Agoraphobia

Not For Sale or Quotation and *dedication to follow.* I am being given a backstage tour. It seems there is a process between books being written and books being read. Who knew?

A note from my editor says 300, or 450, or 600 *words* and a date. I have been given a deadline, a boundary to free up writing.

The *NME* gave me space to write, a different kind of space than the ones that have me running for shelter, hyperventilating, stranded on doorsteps.

The writer Mavis Gallant once observed that 'The distinction between journalism and fiction is the difference between without and within.' Empty within, I will learn to write *without.*

And there is a whole new generation of writers to write about, all American, all bristling with freshly minted energy. Louise Erdrich, Janet Hobhouse, Florence King. The puckish Lorrie Moore, her every line turning highwire somersaults. Jay McInerney and Tama Janowitz, the self-styled slaves of New York. The Valium drawl of a twenty-one-year-old Bret Easton Ellis. I review his novel *Less Than Zero.* Its first line reads: *People are afraid to merge on freeways in Los Angeles.*

An agoraphobe reviewing books about the untrammelled landscapes of America? I'm not unaware of the irony.

That first memory of the moon landing was my birth into an imaginary America. As I grew up I would continue to return there, soothed and enraptured by the stories it told about itself. My local Odeon was like something from the Roman Empire, if the Roman Empire had had deep red carpets and sold popcorn. I sat and watched and listened. I stayed for the credits and wondered at the strange jobs with strange titles: Best Boy, Key Grip, Gaffer. Jobs that sound like racehorses.

In the beginning was the image and the image was American. I surrendered to its enormity, captured like dust motes in a light beam. America was unfettered possibility, a realm of endless self-invention. It was cops and cowboys and air conditioning and steak for breakfast. Perfect teeth, swimming pools, taxi cabs and neon beer signs. Their cities didn't sleep. They had sharp angles.

They spelt 'colour' without the 'u'. Who needed it?

Why bother with the curative countryside when I had the alchemy of CinemaScope? American emptiness was of a different order, an epic scale. The opening of Leone's *Once Upon a Time in the West* – a group of killers waiting for a train in a desert that stretches all the way to infinity. Or Clint Eastwood riding into town on his mule. Or Peter Fonda and his psychedelic Harley. Or James Dean playing chicken in a car whose radio is playing 'There Ain't Nobody Here But Us Chickens'.

America is a culture that seems to understand the aesthetics of agoraphobia. It teaches me a language I didn't know I already knew. 'I take SPACE to be the central fact known to man born in America', wrote the poet Charles Olson in *Call Me Ishmael*: 'I spell it large because it comes large here. Large, and without mercy.'

America: its movies, its music, its writers. My phobia's perverse compensation.

Everything I am not, America allows me to imagine all I could be.

If I had been raised to know my place, Americans didn't seem to know they had one, or one that couldn't be changed by moving. And moving quickly.

'All modern American literature comes from one book by Mark Twain called *Huckleberry Finn*', wrote Ernest Hemingway. *Huck Finn* is the story of a white boy and a black slave both set adrift on a boat on the Mississippi. Both are travelling. The boy is escaping from responsibility, family, citizenship, precisely those things his companion is escaping to. America's founding novel is about the ambivalence inherent in travel, about how movement cuts both ways at once.

Freedom from and freedom to. The word has different colours. Different colors.

I was fourteen when I bought a copy of Kerouac's *On the Road*. A week later I bought my first denim jacket. The cover has a young man – languorous in checked shirt and jeans – propped on the bonnet of a car. He is opening a can of beer, the very measure of rugged male bohemia. 'The Beat Generation's Classic Novel of Sex, Jazz and Freedom' reads the blurb. As though one led to the other. Or were all the same thing.

There are moments in *On the Road* when Sal Paradise – the novel's narrator – experiences such an ecstasy of possibility that he is paralysed, brought to a state of sublime terror: 'the complete step across chronological time into timeless shadows . . . a phantom dogging its own heels, and myself hurrying to a plank where all the angels dove off and flew into the holy void of uncreated emptiness.'

The term 'Beat' was a triple entendre: musical Beat, angelically Beatific, existentially Beaten. By 1958 the *San Francisco*

Chronicle would sneer that these 'bearded cats and kits were . . . only beat, y'know, when it comes to work.'

The paper coined the term Beat-nik, thus implying the poets were communists, coeval with Sputnik – the Russian satellite that triggered the space race. The simple suffix was all it took.

A decade later and Kerouac was sat at home watching TV and drinking Falstaff beer when he started coughing up blood. His liver had exploded after years of alcohol abuse. 'So he drank himself to death,' said his friend the poet Allen Ginsberg, 'which is only another way of living, of handling the pain and foolishness of knowing that it's all a dream, a great, baffling, silly emptiness after all.'

The American writer is the American drinker. It is, by now, a familiar list, a hall of weary infamy. The bullish Norman Mailer, spiritual son of Hemingway, both of them drunks who kept their cocks in the liquor cabinet. Truman Capote and Tennessee Williams, dissipated to the end. John Cheever, his diaries dripping in alcoholic self-disgust. Richard Yates, John Berryman, John Williams, Raymonds Carver and Chandler.

Death, modernity, dread. It don't get more American than that.

In November 1946 the novelist Carson McCullers was on a book tour of Paris, her arrival described by one critic as like a tiny bottle of glass bursting on the French capital. Her publisher arrived at her hotel intending to take her to lunch: 'What I found there was a woman with an oddly childlike air, dressed in a nightgown, still in bed, with a bottle of cognac next to her and a glass of cognac in her hand . . . She did not seem to comprehend me very well. When she had understood, she explained that she could not go out, that she was having an attack of agoraphobia and was consequently incapable of taking two steps in the street.'

Large and without mercy – as applicable to the unquenchable thirst of the alcoholic as it is to the vast plains of Iowa. Alcoholism carves out new spaces inside yourself, excavates bottomless holes of need. It seeks out new borders. It expands and accelerates. Alcoholism is an inner wilderness, a frontierless frontier.

Just how American do you want it?

The myth of creative self-destruction seemed to speak to my generation, the men in particular. It had its roots in Romanticism and its climax in rock 'n' roll. Its inflections are heroic, a defiant response to a world shot through with phoniness and falsity.

On Agoraphobia

Annihilation seemed a small price to pay for a shot at the real, the so-called authentic. Death was an occupational hazard. Madness was crazy and who didn't want that? Crazy meant a deranged soothsaying, waves of ecstatic excess.

That was before I became agoraphobic. My neurosis was intent on moving in the other direction. Implosive rather than expansive. Agoraphobes are the ultimate squares, arch conformists. We fetishise sanity, crave obscene amounts of the stuff.

A phobia is the abnormal pursuit of normality.

Blank

'The point of rooms is that they're inside.'
Don DeLillo, *White Noise*

It is my third year at Warwick. I am twenty-one years old.
I am afraid to merge on motorways. I am afraid to merge.

I am prescribed Ativan, warned about its addictive properties, its short *half-life*, a phrase more descriptive than it
is meant to be. *Half-life* was a term once associated with
nuclear physics and radioactive decay. Now we use it for
tranquillisers, for those whose lives are too much for them.
For whom half a life will have to do. Not that I'm complain-
ing. It is love at first sight. Lazy tongue, heavy eyelids, the
warm release at the back of the neck.

I read the label: *Do not drive. Do not operate machinery.*

Deal.

On Agoraphobia

After three months I am hooked, prescribed Valium, another tranquilliser, to ease the withdrawal.

Agoraphobia is not depression, but live with it long enough and it becomes so. Both have in common the impossibility of feeling anything else.

I am grateful for tranquillisers, for every GP who wrote my every prescription. The Valium dose increases from 5 to 10 to 15 to 20 mgs. The brown plastic bottle has a child-proof lock. On the front are three magical words: *Or As Required*.

When are they not required?

It was called *a script* for a reason. We know how to trot out our lines. The doctor gives me the standard lecture: the dangers of addiction. I give him my supplicant plea:

I know they are addictive but . . . finals

Just get through this term . . . finals

Only using them when I have to . . . finals

That word seems to do the trick. The final word.

Sentences are no less manipulative for being true.

I am the same age as Valium (generic name: diazepam). Patented by a Swiss firm – Hoffmann-La Roche – in 1959 and launched four years later, it was the highest-selling medication in the United States between 1968 and 1982. The economic expansion of the period masked – if not produced – a lingering and concurrent anxiety. In 1978 there were two billion tablets prescribed worldwide. By the mid-1980s its addictive properties were already well known, had been known for years. Tranquillisers were the drug of the affluent society, emotional novocaine guaranteed to take the sting out of the twin obsessions of the time: nuclear war and the nuclear family.

The drug has a cinematic pedigree – suburban housewives numbing their way through an empty marriage, domestic dissatisfaction dulled by a cocktail of mother's little helpers. Say *Valium* and I think American: films like *Diary of a Mad Housewife*, *A Woman Under the Influence*, *The Stepford Wives*. Betty in *Mad Men*. Blurry girls on happy pills.

From campus GP to psychiatric outpatient – a journey of four months, three miles and heavy medication. A man with sideburns and slip-on shoes asks *What have we here?* He writes me a new prescription. One to add to my old prescription.

He gives me the names of people I should talk to.

On Agoraphobia

In *Vacant Possession*, Hilary Mantel's dark farce about the 1980s, a mental-health administrator asks Muriel, the long-term resident of a psychiatric hospital: 'How would you like a new life, with your needs met by the community instead of the institution?'

Such a hopeful question, one phrased in such a way it's difficult to see what the problem might be. Is this not precisely what mental-health reformers had been calling for? An initiative to de-institutionalise the mentally ill and re-integrate them back into the community?

The critic Raymond Williams once noted that 'community' is a word that never seems *to be used unfavourably*. It is *warmly persuasive* and describes *more direct, more total and therefore more significant relationships*.

Community is something it is impossible to be against.

It was assumed that the Family (another word it appears impossible to be against) would come to the rescue, prop up Care in the Community and provide the (often specialised) help that would be needed.

But what of people without families? Or for whom the family had been precisely the problem?

A prefab: the setting for my community mental-health support group. My fellow patients – sorry, *clients* – sit at desks, a parody of a 1950s classroom. Some of them have spent lifetimes being subject to the totalising regimes of psychiatric wards and mental hospitals. They are unable to re-adjust. People with complex histories of long-term medication. Survivors of electroconvulsive therapy, people with violent histories, addiction, domestic abuse and a score of other traumas kept hidden and undiagnosed.

We write things on our yellow notepads, lists of things we want to achieve. What *do* we want to achieve? It is a broad and perplexing question. There is a woman who wants Jesus to stop leaking out of her radiators. An ex-miner who wants a job and his wife to come back to him.

And an agoraphobic young man who wants to be able to venture out into open spaces.

Light

'Melancholy can be overcome only by melancholy.'

Robert Burton, *The Anatomy of Melancholy*

When he was gathering material for *Die Agoraphobie*, Dr Westphal could not have known that nearly four thousand miles away across the Atlantic, in a house in Amherst, Massachusetts, was a woman who is said to have dressed only in white and talked to visitors through closed doors. He could not have read the poetry she was writing, about homes and houses and trembling, or known of the one thousand seven hundred poems she wrote, of which only a handful would be published in her lifetime.

I was sixteen when I first encountered Emily Dickinson and those mysterious statements that were unlike any poetry I had ever read. Her words were like those of the religious mystics: concise, paradoxical, rhapsodic. They seemed to embody the ideas they were expressing, become *the thing itself*. 'Pain has an Element of Blank —': 'I'm nobody! Who are you?': 'I am alive – I guess': 'I heard a Fly buzz – when I died': 'I felt a funeral, in my brain.'

It was the punctuation that first struck me, those dashes that seemed like trip wires, the volcanic capitals and disruptive commas. It is as though language is running to catch up with her, a hyperventilating breath. Her voice inhabits the space between lines. Between words.

Her poetry has stayed with me ever since, re-visited every few years. The various editions have got fatter with age, fed on a diet of Post-it notes and dog-ears; pages the colour of liver spots.

Each generation re-discovers Dickinson, finds in her Protean verse a language that speaks to its own condition. There has been Dickinson the minimalist, the proto-Modernist, a poet whose work aspires to silence. Or Emily as rapturous rock star, her work made a choral symphony in John Adams' *Harmonium*.

'Wild Nights' is the poem on which Adams' music ends: 'Were I with thee/Wild Nights should be/Our luxury.' 'It is like a Mick Jagger lyric,' said Adams about his choice.

On Agoraphobia

As a student it was Dickinson the real-life Madwoman in the Attic, feminist refusenik and insistent nay-sayer. The noughties brought us Queer Dickinson, author of the Master Letters – three unsent expressions of abject masochistic surrender to a figure whose identity still eludes us. There has been Dickinson the Abolitionist, Dickinson the Non-Conformist and Dickinson the Transcendentalist. We have had epileptic Emily, autistic Emily, schizophrenic Emily.

And we have had Emily the agoraphobic.

In his introduction to Dickinson's *Selected Poems* Ted Hughes wrote of a poetry 'solid with metaphor, saturated with the homeliest imagery and experience . . . musical games – of opposites, parallels, mirrors, Chinese puzzles, harmonising and counterpointing whole worlds of reference; and everywhere . . . the teeming carnival of world-life.'

Then: 'Around 1860, something decisive happened to Emily Dickinson.'

This much we know: family of high social standing, material comfort, an unimpeachable Puritan lineage rejected by Emily. Sickly Mother, Domineering Father – a judge, politician and treasurer of Amherst College. ('His Heart was pure and terrible and I think no other like it exists.'

During his funeral she listened to the prayers said for him through a crack in her bedroom door.) Seven years at Amherst Academy – finest education available; excelling at botany, geology and arithmetic as well as Latin and the classics. Strong attachment to older brother Austin. Passionate friendship with sister-in-law Susan Gilbert to whom she wrote hundreds of letters. Fondness for younger sister Lavinia, who would discover the cache of Emily's poems after her death.

In her book *The House Without the Door* Maryanne Garbowsky re-visits Dickinson's story through the DSM – the *Diagnostic and Statistical Manual* produced by the American Psychiatric Association and which (in 1981) included agoraphobia for the first time. There is no shortage of evidence.

Letters to friends from as early as the 1850s report: 'I come and see you a great many times every day, though I don't bring my body.'

Or: 'Sat in Prof Tyler's woods and saw the train move off, and then ran home again for fear somebody would see me, or ask me how I did.'

Or, when in church: 'How big and broad the aisle seemed, full enough before, as I quaked slowly up . . . and there I sat, and sighed, and wondered I was scared so.'

On Agoraphobia

'You speak kindly of seeing me', she wrote to Thomas Wentworth Higginson – an editor at the *Atlantic Monthly* – in June 1869. 'Could it please your convenience to come so far as Amherst I should be very glad, but I do not cross my Father's ground to any House or town.'

By 1870 Emily Dickinson had not left her house for five years. After eight years of correspondence Higginson paid her a visit. There he encountered 'a little plain woman with two smooth bands of reddish hair & a face a little like Belle Dove's . . . She came to me with two day lilies which she put in a sort of childlike way into my hand & said "These are my introduction" in a soft frightened breathless childlike voice – & added under her breath Forgive me if I am frightened; I never see strangers & hardly know what to say – but she talked soon & thenceforward continuously – & deferentially – sometimes stopping to ask me to talk instead of her – but readily recommencing.'

'I was never with anyone who drained my nerve power so much', he later wrote to his wife. 'Without touching me, she drew from me. I am glad not to live near her.'

Spasmodic was the verdict of Higginson on the first batch of poems she sent to him, *uncontrolled*. Her reply is unrepentant: 'You think my gait "spasmodic" – I am in danger Sir – You think me "uncontrolled" – I have no Tribunal.'

Dickinson scholarship has a pathology of its own; it is compelled to read her poetry as possessing the key to her seclusion. *The Long Shadow, Lives Like Loaded Guns, The Riddle of Emily Dickinson, The Passion of Emily Dickinson, The Hidden Life of Emily Dickinson*.

Studies of Dickinson have titles like crime novels, locked-room mysteries.

Dickinson vocabulary: *Prospective, Immensity, Boundlessness, Expanse*.

In *Emily Dickinson and the Image of Home* Emily Mudge calculates that the words *house* or *home* and their cognates appear in 210 poems, about 12 per cent of her known work.

Dickinson is American literature's most enduring ghost story. 'She enjoyed riddles', wrote one of her many biographers, 'apparently enjoyed being one.'

Does diagnosing her with agoraphobia solve the riddle, or simply re-phrase it?

Dickinson became ill with 'Bright's disease' in November 1885 – an ailment of the kidneys characterised by swelling and the presence of albumin in the urine – and died on

On Agoraphobia

15 May 1886. In the instructions for her funeral she asked 'to be carried out the back door, around through the garden, through the opened barn from front to back, and then through the grassy fields to the family plot, always in sight of the house.'

Home Sick

'When they were building the walls,
how could I not have noticed?'
C. P. Cavafy, 'Walls'

Isn't your hometown supposed to feel smaller when you return?

My twenty-first birthday has been and gone. I am back living at home, a graduate if you please. I am told my whole future is ahead of me, a phrase that feels like a threat.

Twenty-one: the key to the door.

So why can I not leave the house?

Doors allow us to negotiate inbetween-ness. They are our answer to being permeable. *When is a door not a door?* One of the earliest jokes I can remember. The meeting of language and thresholds.

As children we would knock on doors and run away, stand on the street corner and wait to see who answered. It seemed astonishing that a mere slab of wood, two inches deep, could separate a cobbled street from the world of firesides and fitted carpets. A parallel world, a mere door's width away.

I open the front door and walk three, four, five steps. The world tilts, spirals, crushes my chest. I turn back. And close the door behind me.

Close the door behind you. It must be one of the most oft-delivered lines on screen. The words guarantee drama, the preface to a sacking, an accusation, plotting and subterfuge. They are the build-up to lines like *this must never leave this office* or *strictly between us*. It is a defining moment. When you shut the door behind you, you know something has gone – is about to go – wrong.

I want to write, but there is no one now to write for. The *NME* has had a change of direction. New owners, new editors. No more *think pieces*, no more vagrant cultural theory, no more free books.

Graham Caveney

I buy the *Guardian* every Monday – *Jobs: Creative, Media and Marketing*. As though those things are interchangeable. Jobs for writers have the word *copy* in front of them. They are all in London. Is living in London part of the writer's job description? I can barely get to the top of my street.

I sit and watch videos: *The Graduate* – Dustin Hoffman's Ben Braddock, icon of educated disaffection. *This is Benjamin* runs the tag line for the poster, *He's a little worried about his future.*

He spends his days floating face down in a swimming pool, his nights in hotel rooms with Mrs Robinson.

My parents do not have a swimming pool. They are helpless before my agoraphobia (is this why I have it?). I have gone from being *a credit* to *a worry*.

Look at the picture of my mother in her headscarf. Look at the doubts flickering at the corner of her eyes. Her indomitable spirit is a cover story for a less heroic life. Her proud ferocity does not extend further than her own social class. It is horizontal.

In arguments she speaks the words of mortal combat: *Over my dead body, not on your life, a cold day in hell.*

On Agoraphobia

No such spleen for the psychiatrist or GP. The professional class demand a softer vocabulary: deferential, apologetic. *Would it be all right if? Don't want to bother you. Sorry to be a nuisance.*

These worlds – these words – are vertical.

They induce vertigo.

Neither do I have a Mrs Robinson. What I have is a video player. My skin is the colour of curdled milk, prison pale. 'We are creatures of light', wrote Ted Hughes, by which he did not mean the luminous tubes of the TV screen.

Hoffman was thirty when he played the twenty-one-year-old Benjamin, Anne Bancroft thirty-five as the fifty-something Mrs Robinson. Such is the barbed promise of Hollywood.

I used to think the word 'deadened' simply meant feeling nothing, an emotional blank. That was before I became deadened.

Deadened isn't like being dead: it is to have a paving stone in your stomach. It is mourning. Grief for the loss of yourself.

I am told I need to expand my *comfort zone*. The phrase used to refer to the climatic temperature. At some point it became a place inside our heads and bodies, a limitation. I'm told it is something good to challenge, something I should try to break out of.

My comfort zone offers me no comfort.

People tell me about their holidays, jobs, the commute to work. They complain about traffic jams, they go for drives in the country. Like it is the most natural thing in the world.

I try walking along the main road, hold on to lampposts, hyperventilate in bus shelters. I test out the path by the canal. My pace quickens when I lose sight of built-up areas. Damp palms, heart like a frightened hare's.

I try not to run but end up running.

There is no shortage of reasons to stay indoors: news stories, weather reports, traffic chaos. Realistic fear allows me to avoid neurotic fear, lends respectability to my avoidance. It means no questions asked, no shameful confession.

On Agoraphobia

My agoraphobia is an irrational dread in search of more rational forms. It will take whatever excuses it can get.

I leave the house at night, let darkness wrap itself around me like a cape. The off-licence doubles as a video shop. It too suffers from a crisis of identity. Not to mention scale: *Three for two, 10% Extra.*

The world is a different size than it is meant to be.

And so I ask again: Isn't your hometown supposed to feel smaller when you return?

Treat

'Though men are not dogs, they should humbly try to
remember how much they resemble dogs
in their brain functions, and not boast
themselves as demigods.'

William Sargant, *Battle for the Mind* (1957)

The last doctor Ford Madox Ford consulted about his agoraphobia told him he would be dead within a month: 'As soon
as he was gone I jumped up, dressed myself and all alone
took a hansom to Piccadilly Circus. You are to remember
that my chief trouble was that I imagined that I could not
walk. Well, I walked backwards and forwards across the
Circus for an hour and half. I kept on saying, "Damn that
brute. I will not be dead in a month."'

The doctor in question would later claim he had provoked
Ford deliberately, goaded the bloody-minded writer into full
recovery. It worked. 'From that day to this', Ford wrote in

Return to Yesterday, 'I have never spent a day in bed. Doctors have occasionally ordered me to but I never manage to get beyond four pm.'

Ford's self-cure was a version of what clinical psychologists would later call *flooding* – a term coined by Dr Isaac Marks, one of the UK's most prolific researchers into agoraphobia. If you have received any treatment for phobias over the past fifty years the chances are it will have been influenced by Marks' work and the behavioural models he helped develop.

'We can wade into cold water bit by bit or just dive in', wrote Dr Marks in his book *Fears, Phobias and Rituals*, 'exposure to fear cues can be gradual, starting with slightly frightening cues and slowly moving to terrifying ones . . . Or it can begin at the top of the hierarchy, with the most alarming first.'

The longest-standing members of my support group – the ones who can date their condition back to the 80s or before – have all encountered flooding at one time or another. The lady with the never-to-be-met grandchildren recalls being taken to Meadowhall shopping centre in Sheffield and made to stay there until her panic peaked. She stayed there for hours.

Except the panic didn't peak. It kept returning in wave after terrifying wave, apparently inexhaustible. She says she felt like a boxer hanging on the ropes, inviting an opponent to punch himself out. She ran away, caught a taxi and has never been back.

She starts to cry as she tells us this, catches herself, laughs instead, says serves her right for agreeing to such a stupid treatment. Flooding? Never trust anything named after a natural disaster.

Both Marks and flooding were products of classic behaviourist thinking. An idea born of the late nineteenth century, an orthodoxy of the mid-twentieth, behaviourism replaced the psychoanalytic couch with the white coat of the laboratory. It promised a scientific model of the human subject. We are, it assured us, the sum of our conditioned responses, reflexes and stimuli. The products of learned behaviour.

There is a now famous experiment carried out by the behaviourist John B. Watson on a nine-month-old infant known as Little Albert. He exposed the child to a variety of stimuli – masks, a rabbit, a white rat, burning newspapers – to which Albert had no response. Watson then combined showing him the rat with banging a metal bar, a noise which made the child cry. After numerous pairings of rat and noise, the child would begin to cry simply by being shown the rat. No noise required; conditioning complete.

From a behaviourist point of view, a phobia is less a disease than a computing error of the central nervous system. We are not ill, just badly programmed. A white rat begins life as a neutral stimulus. It is just a white rat. It is the unconditioned stimulus – the loud bang – that causes fear. Somehow the phobic confuses one with the other, the white rat becomes the conditioned stimulus, fear the conditioned response.

After conditioning, Albert was afraid not just of white rats, but various things white and furry. The sight of Santa Claus' beard reduced him to tears.

Behaviourism casts Little Albert as the prototype of phobics everywhere. We have learned to be afraid of the wrong things, have misread the danger signals. It doesn't matter how or why. The point is to re-educate fearful thinking, to adapt our minds to a new set of responses.

I was offered flooding in the 80s, back when I had returned to live with my parents. I refused it, or rather my agoraphobia refused it on my behalf. It seemed to me then (it seems to me still) the most counter of counter-intuitive treatments, a doublethink, if not a dictatorship, of common sense.

The way to overcome a phobia may well be to expose yourself to it, but exposing yourself to it is precisely the thing you are fearful of. It assumes the sufferer is confident enough to confront their fear to begin with, to trust they will not be destroyed by the process. Flooding only works for those ready to be flooded.

And for those prepared to carry on being flooded, because flooding is only successful when repeated. If a phobia is one long catastrophic habit, overcoming it needs to be equally habitual. We need to spend time with white rats, re-condition ourselves to separate furry rodent from loud scary bang. We need to confront the fear until it no longer feels like fear, until being flooded ceases to be a flood.

The question of consent became just one of flooding's many problems (long-term rates of relapse were another). The sufferer may be certain they want to proceed in the safety of a psychiatrist's office but soon change their mind when faced with the situation in all its phobic horror. I know of one woman who changed her mind and was told she would be forfeiting the right to any further treatment.

On Agoraphobia

The phobic may under-estimate how terrified their phobia makes them feel, have forgotten why they became phobic in the first place. Flooding may well remind them, cause a traumatic re-enactment of their originary drama.

'I'm not running away from my responsibilities,' says Yossarian in Joseph Heller's *Catch*-22: 'I'm running to them. There's nothing negative about running away to save my life.'

Skirting

'[It is] as if the Almighty, in creating the female sex, had taken the uterus and built a woman around it.'

Address to an American medical society, 1870

In *Rumour of Heaven* Beatrix Lehmann (sister of Rosamond) creates a young ballet dancer – Miranda – who had been famous in all the greater European capitals. She marries a promising man of letters, and prepares for life amongst London society: 'And so they lived for several happy dream-like years. And then Clare was born, and Miranda never danced again. It was not because her body had suffered from the advent of the baby, for Miranda never lost her breath-taking beauty of form and face; but she no longer wished to dance. And what was stranger still, she might never have been a dancer nor worn a pair of ballet shoes for all the reference she made to her former glory. She developed an aversion to crowds and noise so that William soon ceased to take her to the theatre, and the gay parties in the

Bayswater house were discontinued. The ponies and the carriage were sold, and Miranda, ecstatically happy with the baby, seldom left the house.'

She has another child. She begins to keep the doors and windows locked; she closes the curtains during daylight: 'She developed a dragging walk and would trail heavily around the house, stopping every now and again to look behind her, puzzled and irritated, searching for the invisible chains that impeded her progress.'

Emma and I have no children. I was raised at a time when people used to whisper about *baby blues*. I used to think they were the name of a pop song. Yet I do know this: pregnancy raises the most fundamental questions about outside and inside, of what belongs where and who it belongs to.

Do medical forms still refer to Date of Confinement?

There was a time when men seem compelled to touch the stomachs of pregnant women whenever they met them. Was this – is this? – a fetish for female liminality, a body that is both autonomous and social?

Of her own experience of agoraphobia the feminist critic Nancy Mairs reflected: 'That at least two-thirds of us are women surprises me not at all. We are the products, individually and collectively, of a cultural tradition of such antiquity that it was already old when the Greek woman was debarred from the agora. We have had to hide while menstruating, cover our heads and swaddle our bodies, lower our eyes, hold our tongues . . . We've known where we belong. And if we've tried to trespass over the threshold, our hearts have knocked, our mouths have gone dry and our skins damp, our lungs have shriveled, our bowels have let go. There's nothing like the symptoms of agoraphobia for keeping a woman in her place. Let me tell you. Nothing.'

At Catholic grammar school we were taught the foetus was an unborn child, that its humanity (and therefore its rights) began at the moment of conception. We were shown pictures of foetuses in jars, each one captioned with the words *This is a baby at* . . . eight, twelve, fourteen weeks.

Thus could we witness God's sanctity evolve, a creation of Him, not the woman to whose body the foetus belonged.

The pregnant woman is sentimentalised into invisibility, banished to the pedestal of myth (earth, virgin, nature). She is revered and reviled, miracle worker and dangerous Hecate: freakishly irrational, hyper-hormonal. When I google Pregnant Woman the first page suggested is *gifts*; it is followed closely by *diet*.

Add *agoraphobia* or *postpartum depression* to the search and a whole new lexicon emerges, one bubbling with barely contained fury.

'I stayed indoors at home for a long time . . . because of the baby,' says Polly Talbot to her doctor in Penelope Gilliatt's novel *One By One*: 'When I went out . . . I honestly didn't expect it would be so difficult . . . I started shaking as soon as I got into the road and I couldn't move. I seemed to pass out . . . It took me weeks to go out again after that time . . . Then I tried going out with the baby to the shops. The first time I was sick. It was worse than I thought.'

Polly is lucky. Her doctor listens, is empathetic. He says: 'We do try, you know. It's a condition that I believe they call the housebound housewife. I'm sorry, is the description unkind?'

What I know of postpartum depression I know through the women in my support group. One of them describes how for nine months she was the centre of her husband's world, feted and fussed over, the mother of his child. She could eat whatever she wanted, sleep in the afternoon. She was big and round and alive. They chose names, clothes, sent scans of her stomach to the in-laws. He sent her texts every day and went with her to antenatal classes. It – she – was a miracle.

And then the baby came, and everything flipped. She felt abandoned, evacuated. She felt she had disappeared.

Another woman tells us how the birth itself had been traumatic, a breech birth, the baby's legs up to its abdomen, its feet next to its ears. She was told it was something to do with the filling of the intrauterine space. She spent seventy-two hours in labour, a cephalic presentation. She says her body was *all wrong*, that childbirth is supposed to be natural, but this felt anything but. It was like being torn apart.

Like being torn apart. A traumatic birth, and the trauma of being born. An originary drama if ever there was one.

When Macduff says he 'was from his mother's womb/ Untimely ripped,' he is referring to his Caesarean birth. It is the line that signals the end for Macbeth, the last of the weird sisters' prophecies: no man of woman born shall harm him. Yet does it not also speak to a more general condition, a sense that we are born too soon?

'With reference to the natural process of childbirth,' remarked the psychologist D. W. Winnicott, 'one thing can seldom be forgotten, the fact that the human infant has an absurdly big head.'

Small hips, big head. We are anatomical misfits.

We are born prematurely, regardless of the length of gestation. Most mammals can walk within hours of being born. Within days they can feed themselves. We cannot walk for fourteen months, remain helpless and vulnerable for years. Maybe we never get over it, the experience of being a bundle of instincts and impulses, appetites and needs.

'To have a body is to learn to grieve', wrote the poet Michael Heffernan in his poem 'In Praise Of It'. It is a line worthy of Emily Dickinson, one that often burbles away when I'm at my most agoraphobic. Some days the words are like a chorus greeting me every time I leave the house. I digest them as I walk down my garden path.

Having a body rather than *being* one. Our physicality a doleful possession, an education in loss.

Catholics have a name for this grief. They call it *original sin*. Psychologists call it something different – the divided self, the shattered ego. Either way the two seem to agree on one thing, a thing agoraphobics know every time they set foot outside their front door: our bodies are much less coherent than we imagine them to be. They reveal us at our most dependent, expose our fantasies of autonomy.

Ghost

'Some women marry houses/It's another kind of skin.'
Anne Sexton, 'Housewife'

In *The Feminine Mystique*, her 1963 polemic about gender relations in the US, Betty Friedan coined the phrase 'The Problem That Has No Name': 'Each suburban housewife struggles with it alone', wrote Friedan. 'As she made the beds, shopped for groceries, matched slipcover material, ate peanut butter sandwiches with the children, chauffeured Cub Scouts and Brownies, lay beside her husband at night – she was afraid to ask even of herself the silent question – "Is this all?"'

Friedan's 'problem without a name' was not agoraphobia. She was diagnosing a much more general malaise, one which seemed to feed off the discontent and dissatisfaction inherent in the gender roles of post-war America. Women, she argued, were complicit in this. She criticised the 'new breed of women writers' who portrayed 'a comic world of children's pranks and eccentric washing machines and Parents' Night at the PTA.' She had in mind the writers for *Good Housekeeping* and *Ladies' Home Journal*, magazines she saw as being a form of feminine minstrelsy.

Friedan singled out the writer Shirley Jackson and her book *Life Amongst the Savages* – a collection of homespun cornball comedies of the kind that sold mind-numbing amounts in the 50s and early 60s. 'Do real housewives then dissipate in laughter their dreams and their sense of desperation?' asked Friedan: 'Do they think their frustrated abilities and their limited lives are a joke?'

Shirley Jackson's life was anything but.

In the *New Yorker* of June 1948 Jackson had published 'The Lottery' – a short story about an imagined modern-day stoning ritual in a New England village. It made her famous virtually overnight. Readers wrote in their hundreds – outraged, puzzled, offended, excited, deeply concerned. Some cancelled their subscriptions. Others were curious about where such rituals took place. They wanted to know if they could go and watch.

Four months later Jackson arrived at a hospital in Vermont to give birth to her third child. The admissions clerk asked her to state her occupation. *Writer*, said Jackson.

Housewife, said the clerk.

Writer, Jackson repeated.

I'll just put down housewife, said the clerk.

A woman's place is in the home – the desperate tagline of the fifties. Which meant homes were anything but homely. Homes were uncanny, unsettling, unheimlich. *The Road Through the Wall*, *We Have Always Lived in the Castle*, *The Haunting of Hill House*. The titles of Jackson's novels read as one embittered cry against the imprisoning expectations – the dualities and internal exile – of post-war American femininity. They make up some of the most disturbing horror fiction since Poe, a taut domestic Gothic.

Of writing her novels she said: 'I find a wall surrounding some forbidden, lovely secret, and in this wall a gate that cannot be passed . . . I had set myself up nicely within the wall inside a big strange house I found there, locked the gates behind me, and discovered that the only way to stay there with any degree of security was to destroy, utterly, everything outside.'

Jackson's biography reads like the best of her fiction. Unwanted daughter of a domineering mother (she told her she was the result of a failed abortion), the college breakdown, unhappy marriage to a man resentful of his wife's success but who was dependent on her income. The overeating, the diet pills, the booze.

She claimed to have magical powers (surely a symptom of the disempowered). She dabbled in voodoo and Tarot, claimed that she had put a curse on the publisher Alfred Knopf that had caused him to break a leg. The dust jacket of her first novel described her as 'the only contemporary writer who is a practising amateur witch.' One reviewer named her Virginia Werewolf.

She in turn named her moods, developed them as though they were separate people – 'sharly (snarly shirley) and shurly (surly shirley)'. She wrote in her diary of 'that compound of creatures I call Me.' Interviewers spoke of 'the two Miss Jacksons'.

In her biography of Jackson – *A Rather Haunted Life* – Ruth Franklin traces her subject's agoraphobia: an anxiety attack in a New York shopping mall; the husband's affair with her best friend; a fall on the ice twisting her ankle leaving her unable to drive the car.

She was in her mid-forties: 'Shirley stayed inside. Something new and unpleasant had begun to happen every time she tried to leave the house. She would begin to shake, her legs would give way, and everything would start spinning. If she did not go inside right away, she feared passing out . . . Eventually her anxiety was no longer associated only with leaving the house: anything could trigger a panic attack, even the phone ringing.'

She barely left home for the next three years, surviving on a diet of Dexamyl, barbiturates, Miltown and alcohol. She was trying to write another novel, 'a happy book' about a woman starting a new life. Franklin quotes her diaries: 'i cannot write about what i am going to call my obsession because i simply cannot bring myself to put down the words. i don't think that this is a refusal to face it because heaven knows i have thought recently about very little else, but i do think that being unable to write about it is a clear statement by my literary conscience . . . that i know the problem is not real, is imaginery . . . and i cannot in good faith write about it as though it were real, the emotion – let me see – is shame . . . is it painful to write? i thought it was getting better and then it got worse, but it *can* get better, i know.'

It didn't get better. Jackson died in her sleep. She was forty-eight. The subheadings in her *New York Times* obituary read: 'Housework Came First.' Franklin again quotes her final diaries. The subject is divorce but she could as easily have been writing about her agoraphobia: 'to be separate, to be alone, to stand and walk alone, not to be different and weak and helpless and degraded . . . and shut out, not shut out, shutting out.'

The diary ends with a single repeated phrase:

'laughter is possible laughter is possible laughter is possible'.

Vampire

'But is he who opens a door and he who
closes it the same being?'
Gaston Bachelard, *The Poetics of Space*

In the film *Copycat* Sigourney Weaver plays a forensic
psychologist whose expertise in serial killers leads to her
becoming the target of one. She survives but becomes paralysed by fear every time she tries to leave her apartment.
Each attempt is met by a soundtrack of screeching violins.
She cannot collect the newspaper when it is left on the landing. She is, she explains, one agoraphobic asshole. When
detectives call round to ask for her help on a case she begins
to hyperventilate, experiences a full-blown agoraphobic
panic attack.

Because any space can be a public space. Even your own
front room.

My room has a kettle, wash basin, single bed, desk, book-shelves, TV and video player. I am twenty-two years old. I have everything I need.

There are movie posters on the wall. Natasha Kinski in a pink woollen dress cut low across the shoulders. I watch the opening twenty minutes of *Paris, Texas* until the tape is cigarette-paper thin. Harry Dean Stanton is walking across the plains of East Texas. He has haunted cheekbones, an affectless gaze. He is wearing a suit and tie, a red baseball cap. His walk is part military march, part ballet. The sound of Ry Cooder's guitar slices up the vast vacant landscape.

I check my pockets for medication, the miniature bottle of vodka I keep in my jacket.

Travis is the name of Dean Stanton's character – a nod to that other terminal outsider, Travis Bickle, the De Niro of Scorsese's *Taxi Driver*.

It sometimes feels like I spent the whole of my adolescence reciting De Niro soliloquies: *You talking t' me? Whassamadda-wichyou? Get da fuck outta here.*

I could speak the words with a fluency I never had for my native tongue. I sit and watch those films again. It seems those words are speaking me.

On Agoraphobia

Takeaway food, my only contact with the world outside. The delivery driver picks up video tapes as part of the service. No extra charge. I am his best customer.

When the detective asks Sigourney Weaver if the brandy she sips all afternoon *helps any?* Weaver takes a long and bitter pause and says with all the malice in her soul: You don't feel fear, do you?

The food tastes better in the dark. I spoon-feed myself sticky, gloopy sauce straight from the carton. I turn on the bedside lamp to smoke, stare at the wispy trail of grey.

Sigourney Weaver gets cured in a most involuntary fashion. Her would-be killer abducts her, takes her back to the scene of his first failed attempt. She is hanging in a toilet cubicle, her neck one wrong step away from being snapped. The detective must surely come to the rescue.

At around 4.40 each morning I wake to a sudden jolt. *Don't be so fucking stupid. Imagine the outside is just an extension of the inside. Be normal, be normal, be normal.*

I look up the word in my dictionary. *Normal: Standing at right angles; perpendicular.*

I could coach football in Brazil, join a monastery in Japan.

Sigourney and the bad guy slug it out on a rooftop in San Francisco. 'Looks like I cured your agoraphobia,' he says to her, before taking a round to the chest.

I awake with concrete in my stomach, the fear of a breakdown that has already occurred. Thoughts intrude, hover. Thoughts that have lives of their own.

Sigourney walks away at the end of the movie, her red dress and immaculately mussed hair a picture of Hollywood at its most seductive. She reminds me of Joan Crawford, the imperious stride, the upward tilt of the chin.

The credits roll and I stare once more at those job titles: Fixer, Foley Artist – jobs that sound vaguely illegal.

Dawn

'If I possessed the impossible landscapes,
what would remain of the impossible?'

Fernando Pessoa, *The Book of Disquiet*

He puts on his overalls, donkey jacket, boots with dried mud
on them. It is just about light. He makes sandwiches (*fixes
his snap*), puts them in his satchel, grabs his toolbox. He
smells of work – paint, creosote, dust – this man who loves
but can no longer bear me.

Mornings belong to my father, his time away from the chatter of his wife, the worry of his son.

I have yet to go to bed, have not slept today.

The today that is now yesterday.

To be agoraphobic is to be permanently jet-lagged, the on-going fatigue of temporal disruption. It damages our internal clock, those endogenous timers known as circadian rhythms – *circa* meaning 'about', *dies* meaning 'day'. An approximation of a day; the complement to a tranquillised half life.

This clock has receptors – oscillators – which are set to the external world. They are modulated by the light/dark cycle, by sunlight and temperature. They determine our feeding and sleeping patterns, our brain-wave activity, hormone production, the repairing of our DNA.

My mother was right: it is a sin – an offence against our nature – to be indoors on days like this.

She tidies around me as I sit smoking at the kitchen table, stuffs my clothes into a laundry basket. She is appalled. She rarely sleeps later than seven in the morning, and never in the afternoon.

Unable to cure her son, she will clean the house instead.

You must try and have faith.

Yes, but I haven't.

On Agoraphobia

But you must try.

I can't.

Why not?

Because I don't.

Agoraphobia wraps up its sufferer's frustrations in bundles of barbed wire. Probe too long and you will get cut. Beneath the timidity, rage.

And beneath the rage a sorrow so deep you may drown.

How's your agoraphobia? My parents' question fills me with fury. *My* agoraphobia? As if it belonged to me. I test the sentence out: 'I have *got* agoraphobia.' It sounds ridiculous.

I try out different words:

Afflicted by – overripe, predestined somehow.

Developed – like a photograph? Too clinical.

Vanquished, invaded by – militaristic, misses the intimacy.

Surrendered, succumbed, possessed – a heroine from some nineteenth-century novel? Maybe.

I think of Charlotte Brontë's *Villette*: 'Two hot rooms thus became my world,' says Lucy Snowe, 'I forgot that there were fields, woods, rivers, seas, an ever-changing sky . . . All within me became narrowed to my lot.'

Home visits, a new shrink. He asks me what a cure might look like. I picture dome-shaped roofs covering the length of every open road. Chemists every quarter of a mile. The traffic consisting entirely of caravans, their windows blacked out.

I somehow expect him to say, *You're fine, it has all been a terrible misunderstanding.*

He doesn't.

But it is.

My phobia is a terrible misunderstanding.

New shrink means new meds. Benzodiazepines are now supplemented by tricyclic antidepressants, so called because of their three-ring chemical structure. They boost the activity of neurotransmitters – chemicals such as noradrenaline and serotonin – chemicals which affect the regulation of mood. They carpet-bomb the chemistry of the brain, despite there being no evidence that depression – let alone agoraphobia – is caused by chemical imbalance.

Meds open gaps between symptoms and the awareness of symptoms. They instil a perplexed nonchalance, an unenlightened Zen. What once seemed complex emotions now seem a series of flattened emotions all layered on top of each other. Inside the packet a warning: *may cause weight loss, weight gain, insomnia, blurred vision, tremor, epilepsy, movement disorder, mood swings, vomiting, impotence, hot or dry skin, paranoid delusions, hallucinations, suicidal thoughts. If symptoms persist notify doctor.*

How long is *persist*?

Five weeks?

Six months?

Thirty-plus years?

Optics

'I have no house only a shadow.'
Malcolm Lowry, *Under the Volcano*

Amongst the copious notes made by Dr Westphal about one of his early patients – Mr C, a commercial traveller – we find the following observations: 'The use of beer or wine also allowed the patient to pass through the feared locality with comparative comfort.' And again: 'The condition is worse in the mornings when he is sober; the pleasure of only a few glasses of wine or beer eases him greatly.'

Was Mr C an alcoholic for whom attacks of agoraphobia were part of withdrawal? Or an agoraphobic for whom alcohol was a form of self-medication?

And, if the latter, was there a point at which being *eased greatly* turned into dependency?

On Agoraphobia

I am getting ready to go out. I check my jeans pockets: keys, money, tranquillisers. Jacket pocket: wallet, cigarettes, hip flask full of vodka. I am twenty-three years old and I am a functioning alcoholic.

Alcoholism and agoraphobia – a case study in cause and effect. They intersect, interweave, shadow-box. Each other's remedy, each other's poison.

Drinking was a cure for my agoraphobia, even as it became the cause thereof. Alcohol was the acceptable face of self-medication. It was socially sanctioned, government sponsored, available without prescription.

Today psychiatrists talk of *dual diagnosis* – the process by which self-cures become their own disease.

Until recently it was difficult enough to get them to believe in a single diagnosis.

Using alcohol as a coping strategy works. It can work right up until the moment it kills you. It cloaks your fears in hazy indifference, allows you to perform a version of the person you think you could be. Thus are you both more and less authentic, never quite *yourself* – this elusive thing you have heard so much about.

Alcohol introduces you to people for whom it also works – people who rely on it more than you do. You like these people. You share notes, indulge in regular bouts of mutual reassurance. You take comfort in the comparison.

Addiction is a copying as well as a coping strategy.

This is not a book about alcoholism, but it is a book written by an alcoholic. I have spent years talking to recovering drunks and I have yet to find one for whom the experience was one of excess pleasure. Instead, I've found people who needed an extra layer of skin, insulation.

Sober alcoholics like to banish ambivalence from their story, tend to shy away from nuance. They never say *my name is X and, amongst other things, I am an alcoholic.* I can see why. Those *other things* might get in the way. Nuance is a luxury recovery cannot afford. We are making a coherent story out of an incoherent experience. Order out of chaos. We stick to the story because it makes sense – the thing the turbulent life of addiction resists.

The thing that life itself resists.

Dry or drunk? Victim or survivor? Click *Like* or *Dislike*. As though the two are separate categories, unable to coexist.

Are not in fact dependent on each other. And dependent on who is asking. And when they are asking. And why.

Victim or survivor? Triumph or tragedy? Choose your brand.

It depends: the answer to all enquiries regarding my mental health. Yet *It Depends* is never an option on the CBT questionnaires. Or on the forms from government departments wanting to know *how your condition affects your ability to seek work*. (And for whom *It Depends* is always an unacceptable answer.)

And so I cling to the disease model of addiction. Wouldn't you? Spend time with an end-of-the-road drinker and tell me they are not ill. I will certainly take 'illness' over the other available descriptions that have come my way: weakness of character, moral laxity, failure of willpower. I say *it's an illness* and roll out the stats on genetic predisposition, as though families were purely biological factors, not social institutions at all.

I talk about *addictive personality*, as if our personalities are as fixed as our eye colour.

And yet I know it is not that simple. The recovery industry knows this too and has learned to speak out of both sides of its mouth. The disease model of addiction is more precarious than anyone is letting on, but I guess it is a hell of a lot easier – cheaper – than treating its myriad causes.

Alcoholics *do* inherit their condition, but we inherit it from our socio-economic history as well as our DNA.

Alcohol was as much a part of my culture as the King Cotton that put food on our table. It helped wash the dust from our throats. Drinking was medication: whisky for colds, Benedictine and brandy for indigestion. Pregnant women drank stout.

Drinking completed us. Completed us by diminishing us.

Getting drunk was a rite of passage, an initiation into certified manhood. We got *battered*, *steaming*, *slaughtered*, *wrecked*, *hanging*, *stewed*, *shitfaced*, *legless*. We drank before food, with food, as food. We drank in order to have sex. We drank instead of sex. We drank to celebrate and commiserate, to get wound up and then wind down. Drink made us fight, laugh, fuck.

And then, when it had made us ill, we used it to make us feel better.

When psychiatry failed, alcohol came to the rescue. How could it not? It seemed the sensible option. Drinking culture was already available, my birthright. Like those empty fields and stark valleys, alcohol had been there for ever.

Narratives of addiction are a genre like any other, they conform to the classic three-act structure: set up, confrontation, resolution. We are in pain. We fall in love with the thing that eases the pain. That thing then causes pain of its own. Addiction is a story of betrayal.

I used to think agoraphobia was the reason I drank. If I could only solve the cause of my drinking – rid myself of the fear that underpinned it – then the drinking itself would cease to be a problem. Except it does not work like that. It does not work *anything like* that. A drunken agoraphobic is still an agoraphobic. They have simply added alcoholism to their repertoire.

Box

'I want to go back to Room.'

Emma Donoghue, *Room*

All detox units are the same. Plexiglas. Reception. CCTV. A corridor of un-lockable single rooms, an office marked Medical Personnel Only. A TV lounge with stained carpets, stacks of DVDs, jigsaws with missing pieces, spine-broken mystery novels. A kitchen with work surfaces covered in spilled sugar, stained coffee cups, opened packets of biscuits.

They smell of bleach, stale sweat, ammonia, boiled food and bandages.

Let us imagine one such ward, an amalgamation of wards that exist across the North of England. Let us call this ward Flatland, in honour of a novel I read years ago about a world where everything exists in two dimensions.

On Agoraphobia

I am forty-four years old, a once-functioning alcoholic who can no longer function. I have an extended liver, jaundice and acute pancreatitis. I experience a permanent tremor, epileptic seizures and delirium tremens. My hallucinations include: lizards, mice and rats.

Until being admitted, I had not left my house for six months. I have been living off yoghurt drinks and vodka. Dead people sometimes call me on the telephone.

I have lost count of the number of times I've been to Flatland, but it must be close to a dozen. I average one visit every couple of years, intermittent asylum-seeking, each more disheartening than the last. I have become fluent in detox-ese: the bag search (no aftershave or mouthwash), the rubber ball of the blood-pressure machine, the vitamin injections, the daily breathalyser.

The rattle the seasoned drunks call it, describing the first seventy-two hours. The crippling pains in the fibres and joints, the film of cold sweat basting the body. The shakes, the vomiting, the shitting.

By day four I am ready to try solid food. Sloppy solids: soups, porridge, custard. I eat three times a day – same time as the meds. It is the medication not the food I look forward to.

Clomethiazole, brand name Heminevrin. They smell faintly of urine and cause riotous attacks of sneezing twenty minutes after taking them.

Meds leave me fuzzy, weightless, one of those spacemen I had been told were the future. They alleviate anxiety by smothering it, like spraying deodorant on a bad smell.

The doctor gradually decreases the dose. She does not want me swapping one addiction for another. I must withdraw from the pills used to help me withdraw from alcohol. I'm detoxing from the detox.

Sugar is my new fix. I hoover it up. Three spoonfuls per mug of tea. Fizzy pop. Mountains of Maltesers, Fruit Pastilles, boiled sweets. My teeth are not to be reckoned with.

Rehabilitation units are what the sociologist Erving Goffman called *total institutions* – a phrase he coined to describe a place of residence where *like-situated individuals, cut off from the wider society for an appreciable period of time, together lead an enclosed, formally administered round of life*.

In his classic study, *Asylums* (1961), Goffman identified the various strategies used to bring about a new structuring of self, a 'cure' whose efficacy is measured by compliance.

On Agoraphobia

Key to this process was the case record, a document kept by medical staff. The case record details patient behaviour, does so in a way which formalises what is already known about their psychiatric history. The idea is to get the two things to coalesce, for the story to add up to a unified whole. The case record becomes the official story, internalised and inevitable. The asylum's job is to teach us how to tell it.

Group therapy. The counsellor tells us we share a common problem, that our recovery will follow the same twelve steps. We disrespectfully beg to differ. We compete over the severity of our respective addictions, indulge in endless games of one-downmanship. Some speak jail-speak: *On the out, going on the numbers*. It is a world of exclusive codes. It reminds me of the dens I had as a child.

It's a rigged game, says Jack Nicholson's Randle McMurphy in *One Flew Over the Cuckoo's Nest*. He's right, of course. The game is rigged before it has even started, rigged by the same factors that got most of us here: sexual abuse, domestic violence, familial neglect. Add unemployment, poor housing and prison to the mix and it is difficult to see how the game could get any fairer soon.

Of the twelve patients treated in this, my last – my definitive – rehab, only two of us would still be sober a year later. The rigging *is* the game.

Therapy consists of sullen, monosyllabic exchanges, resentment burning beneath each one. We write down the ways in which we are powerless over our addiction. We make gratitude lists, itemising five things we are grateful for.

Or feel we should be grateful for.

Fail to mention *sobriety* on this list and the question comes: *Haven't you forgotten something?*

'If the psychiatric faction is to impress upon him its views about his personal make-up', wrote Goffman, 'then they must be able to show in detail how their version of his past and their version of his character hold up much better than his own . . . The patient must insightfully come to take, or affect to take, the hospital's view of himself.'

I am allowed phone calls, have stopped shaking enough to be able to hold a pen. I write to my oldest friend Dave H, tell him I'm back in Flatland. A single line lifted from Britney Spears: *Oops I did it again.*

I try reading literature but the words blur, collapse on the page. I no longer have the stamina for those great American novels that once were my refuge. Dave writes back, encloses a parcel of books. He has opted for short-story writers, the miniaturists of everyday tragedy: Jayne Anne Phillips, Bobbie Ann Mason.

Rehab is the right place to read them, these laureates of disappointment. Their characters seem permanently lost, drifters rather than pioneers. They have temporary jobs in scrapyards, their pick-up trucks are forever breaking down. Thus is the myth of the American road punctured. No *novels of jazz, sex and freedom* these, but lives that are solitary, broken, quietly despairing. Characters who have stepped out of an Edward Hopper painting.

The narrator of Phillips' 'Fast Lanes' wakes up in a truck with a man whose name she can't quite remember. Her dress still smells of rum. She is trying to piece together the chronology of last night's blackout. She feels dazed, sick, weightless. She turns to the man in the truck and asks him the question she's been meaning to ask for a while: *Where are we?*

I stand in the hospital car park and wait for my taxi. I have a canvas bag containing pyjamas, toiletries and two paperback books. In my pocket is a printout of medical stats, including those of my last liver function blood test. It is an obscene amount, roughly 3500% more than it should be. The doctor says it will decrease over time, that the liver, unlike our other visceral organs, has an incredible ability to repair itself.

Incredible but not infinite. There comes a point when the liver is no longer able to regenerate, where renewal ceases to be an option. That place is a bad place, the doctor says: Believe me, you do not want to go there.

I do believe her. For the first time in twenty-odd years, I am more frightened by alcohol than I am by agoraphobia.

I've spent fourteen days in Flatland, fourteen less than what the doctors recommend, but long enough to convince me: Drinking is no longer an option. Ever.

I will have to begin everything again.

Lines

'Reality is as thin as paper and betrays with all its cracks its imitative character.'

Bruno Schulz, *The Street of Crocodiles*

We are getting ready to go out. Emma puts on her brown tweed skirt and matching jacket, a red polo neck. She stands in front of the mirror, makes last-minute touches to her face. *Putting on her armour*, she calls it.

Manchester city centre on a Saturday spring morning, the weather crisp and cold. Market Street is dotted with stalls: fast food, cancer charities, animal welfare, Jehovah's Witnesses, hats with hearts on them saying *I Love Manchester*.

The crowd is an amorphous body. It has arteries, limbs, a pulse.

It has been over a decade since I was last in Flatland. Ex-drunk: I prefer it to *recovering alcoholic*, less dramatic. But still, a hyphen that saved my life.

Ten years of sobriety have cleared the debris, helped me get rid of the psychic static. *Accept the things I cannot change, change the things I can, hope to know the difference.* I used to say AA's serenity prayer through clenched teeth. I mistook its simplicity for banality. But keep saying it long enough and it starts to take hold. Like St Augustine said: kneeling *is* the prayer.

And now that I no longer depend on alcohol to ease my phobia, it seems it has become less pronounced, even manageable. I work around it. I google all my unknown journeys, work out routes that will keep me safe, find ways to minimise exposure.

I go out every day, particularly on days I don't want to go out. Behaviour needs to be habitual, a muscle in need of exercise. The shrinks were right about that much.

I have taken up yoga. And no, I cannot believe I have typed that sentence either. I resisted it to begin with, was suspicious even after I knew it was working. The language was the problem, the *namaste* and the *fascia* and those sentences that begin *We in the West tend to* . . . Yet yoga is what I do: yin yoga, three times a week.

We make shapes, take poses, hold them. It is another kind of space. It teaches me that emptiness can also be stillness.

I have still not been on a motorway, nor walked round Cheshire's Golden Triangle. I may never get to see Kafka's birthplace in Prague or go to the Pessoa museum in Lisbon. Emma tells me I'm ahead of the game, that I have the smallest carbon footprint of anyone she knows.

We walk past the cathedral and up to the second-hand bookshop. Students bump into us, their eyes locked on screens. I am not the only one with problematic spatial awareness.

The shop's owner has a prosthetic hand and gives you fruit if you spend more than a fiver. I buy a Penguin copy of Lewis Carroll's *Alice* books, stories which as a child I'd shunned as being for children.

Through the Looking-Glass was first published in 1871, the same year as *Die Agoraphobie*. I wonder what Westphal and Charles Dodgson would have made of each other, the intellectual sparring between them. I imagine them playing chess.

A German psychiatrist and an Oxford mathematician. Two very different kinds of men, yet both compelled to tell stories about space and time and the various rabbit holes that lurk therein.

When Alice tells the White Queen that she can't remember things before they happen, the Queen replies *It's a poor kind of memory that only works backwards*, she can remember *things that happened the week after next*.

Remembering the future, the paradox of phobia. The *what if* unable to escape the tyranny of *what was*.

We tell ourselves stories in order to live. No memoir is complete without Joan Didion's much-quoted line. Yet I am drawn to the sentences later on in the paragraph where she writes: 'We interpret what we see, select the most workable of the multiple choices. We live entirely . . . by the imposition of a narrative line upon disparate images, by the ideas with which we have learned to freeze the shifting phantasmagoria.'

On Agoraphobia

Here is a much trickier proposition, the issue of how we interpret the stories we tell. How we re-read them. What we use stories to do and allow to do to us.

We walk down to St Peter's Square and sit on a bench opposite the library. I watch the trams rattle their way to places whose names I grew up with. They still sound clunky, awkward, a bricolage of clipped consonants and hard vowels: Chorlton-cum-Hardy, Ashton-under-Lyne, East Didsbury.

I close my eyes and listen to the sound of voices passing by. Chatter and laughter, one continuous flow.

I tell my students the job of life-writing is not to recount 'interesting lives', but to find interesting ways to describe the lives they already lead, that life-writing is about sentences rather than adventures.

I tell them to put question marks over the definitive story.

A memoirist is not a lawyer, but on this much the two agree: beware the statement that is too consistent.

When I sued the Marist Order – the wing of the Catholic Church to whom my abuser belonged – my agoraphobia became evidence; a story in the world, not just my own head.

For three years I swam amongst the language of the law, became expert on the differences between *causation* and *correlation*, on *what constitutes a material contribution towards* . . .

We said: *My agoraphobia was a result of abuse.*

They said: *What about agoraphobics who have not been abused?*

And besides, isn't your client a recovering alcoholic?

The law is a clinician. Its building blocks are timelines, dates and witness statements, the aim to iron out all ambiguities. It looks for certainty, prides itself on specificity. It needs a credible story about incredible events; its talk of *balance of probabilities* and *particulars of claim* expresses an anxiety about its own limitations.

The law is like an unreliable narrator posing as an omniscient one.

The process taught me just how slippery our stories can be, capricious and slanted. We like to think of our lives as linear, as though they progress from a to b; we're the heroes and heroines of our own personalised novels. We speak in the codes of realism: character, cause and effect, the world faithfully represented.

Yet we know this version does not quite fit, that it is framed and shaped, sculpted. Our stories are customised myths, they paper over the cracks. If we mistake them for The Truth and Nothing But – we risk becoming like Nabokov's gorilla, imprisoning ourselves within them.

I am agoraphobic – the sentence still strikes me as absurd, a punchline to an in-joke I'm not sure I'm in on.

My suspicion of the sentence is part of the problem, a fear of being stranded in someone else's syntax. I'm suspicious of self-definitions generally, though I know how crucial it can be to have them. I'm an alcoholic, I'm a survivor, I'm an agoraphobe.

All of the above, and amongst other things.

Amongst other things – maybe the unwritten subtitle to the genre of memoir itself. Lives are messy, contingent and mysterious. Our stories about them should never be too neat, but disrupt and surprise, make us as different to ourselves as we are to others. To do so is not to disown our experience but to celebrate its magic, to acknowledge that our lives owe as much to the fairytale as the realist novel. Freezing the shifting phantasmagoria makes it no less phantasmagoric.

'I'm afraid I can't explain myself, sir,' says Alice to the Caterpillar, 'because I'm not myself, you see?'

Bibliography

General:

Gaston Bachelard: *The Poetics of Space* (Penguin, 1964)

Paul Carter: *Repressed Spaces: The Poetics of Agoraphobia* (Reaktion Books, 2002)

Karen DeCrow and Robert Seidenberg: *Women Who Marry Houses: Panic and Protest in Agoraphobia* (McGraw-Hill, 1983)

George Frederick Drinka: *The Birth of Neurosis: Myth, Malady, and the Victorians* (Simon and Schuster, 1984)

Terry J. Knapp, Michael Schumacher: *Westphal's 'Die Agoraphobie': The Beginnings of Agoraphobia* (University Press of America, 1988)

Nancy Mairs: *Plaintext: Essays* (University of Arizona, 1992)

Kathryn Milun: *Pathologies of Modern Space: Empty Space, Urban Anxiety, and the Recovery of the Public Self* (Routledge, 2007)

Sue Prideaux: *Edvard Munch: Behind the Scream* (Yale University Press, 2005)

Janet Oppenheim: *Shattered Nerves: Doctors, Patients, and Depression in Victorian England* (OUP, 1991)

Elaine Showalter: *The Female Malady: Women, Madness and English Culture, 1830–1980* (Virago, 1985)

Andrew Thacker: *Moving Through Modernity: Space and Geography in Modernism* (Manchester University Press, 2009)

Anthony Vidler: *Warped Space: Art, Architecture, and Anxiety in Modern Culture* (MIT, 2000)

Elizabeth Wilson: *The Sphinx in the City: Urban Life, the Control of Disorder, and Women* (University of California, 1991)

Individual Writers:

Emily Dickinson:
The Complete Poems (Faber, 1970)
Poems Selected by Ted Hughes (Faber, 1968)
Helen McNeil: Emily Dickinson (Virago, 1986)

Maryanne M. Garbowsky:
The House Without the Door: A Study of Emily Dickinson and the Illness of Agoraphobia (Associated University Press, 1989)

Ford Madox Ford:
Return to Yesterday (Carcanet, 1999)
Parade's End (Wordsworth Classics, 2013)

Max Saunders:
  Ford Madox Ford: A Dual Life (OUP, 1996)

Shirley Jackson:
  all of her works have now been re-issued as Penguin
  Modern Classics
  Ruth Franklin: *Shirley Jackson: A Rather Haunted Life*
  (Liveright, 2016)

Ernest Raymond: *The Autobiography of David*
  (Victor Gollancz, 1946)

Acknowledgements

I am grateful to everyone at Picador, particularly Nicholas Blake, Alice Dewing and Ravi Mirchandani. I am especially grateful to Ansa Khan Khattak. I could not have asked for a sharper, more astute editor. She encouraged this book when it was still an idea and helped me bring it all the way home. It is a pleasure and an education to work with her.

Thanks to Tony Peake – my agent for more years than I care to remember – and to Sally Holloway at Felicity Bryan for so comfortably filling his shoes after his retirement.

After twenty years of living here, Nottingham has become my adopted home. It is a city kind to its writers, and this is due in no small part to the work of Ross Bradshaw and the staff at Five Leaves Bookshop, as well as the indefatigable efforts of David Belbin, Sandeep Mahal, Leanne Moden and Matt Turpin at Nottingham UNESCO City of Literature. Thanks to them all.

I am grateful to the Society of Authors, whose funding enabled me to finish writing the book.

On Agoraphobia

For kindness and conversation I am indebted to: Alan Baker, Kathy Bell, Johnny Bishop, Russell Christie, Jonathan Coe, Hilary Cook, Sarah Dale, Mark Dapin, Joel Davie, Sue Dymoke, Brendan Flanagan, Caroline Hennigan, Fiona Heron, Dave Hesmondhalgh, Julie Hesmondhalgh, David Imrie, Ian Kershaw, Rebecca Kidd, Viji Kuppan, Veronica Layunta-Maurel, Katrina Levi, John Lucas, Maggie MacLure, Eve Makis, Jade Moore, Rob Murphy, Helen Naylor, Deirdre O'Byrne, Yvonne Patrick, Heather Perkins, Mark Russell, Frank and Anja Rutten, Mahendra Solanki, Martin Stannard, Nick Stevenson, Helen Steward, Harry Torrance and Colin Wright.

And finally I want to thank my partner, Emma Robertson, whose suggestion the project first was. This book is dedicated to her.

GC